The
Gwent
Village Book

THE VILLAGES OF BRITAIN SERIES

Other counties in this series include

Most are published in conjunction with
County Federations of Women's Institutes

The
Gwent
Village Book

Compiled by the Gwent
Federation of Women's Institutes from notes
and illustrations sent by Institutes in the County

Published jointly by
Countryside Books, Newbury
and
GFWI, Usk

First Published 1994
© Gwent Federation of Women's Institutes 1994

Countryside Books
3 Catherine Road
Newbury, Berkshire

ISBN 1 85306 312 6

Produced through MRM Associates Ltd., Reading
Typeset by The Midlands Book Typesetting Co.
Printed in England by J. W. Arrowsmith Ltd., Bristol

Foreword

Gwent is a county of beauty, surprises and contrasts. Its mountains rise in the north west to nearly 2,000 feet (600 m); its hill slopes and hidden valleys, rolling farmland and forested uplands give way to coastal levels along the mouth of the Severn.

These contrasts are reflected in the lives of the people who live here. As a border county, Gwent offered relatively easy access to invaders and more peaceful incomers, who have through the ages left their mark on the region in place-names, ancient roads and fortresses, buildings and industrial development.

Gwent has enjoyed only a short life as a modern county, though the name is of ancient Welsh origin. It applied to the south eastern region of Wales until the time of Henry VIII, when Monmouthshire was created and the area became increasingly anglicised. After little more than 20 years of new life, Gwent seems likely soon to see its contrasting areas come under five new unitary authorities: Newport, Monmouth, Torfaen, Caerphilly and Heads of the Valleys.

It is with great pleasure and pride that the Gwent Federation of Women's Institutes has prepared the material for the Gwent Village Book.

Marguerite Shaw
County Chairman

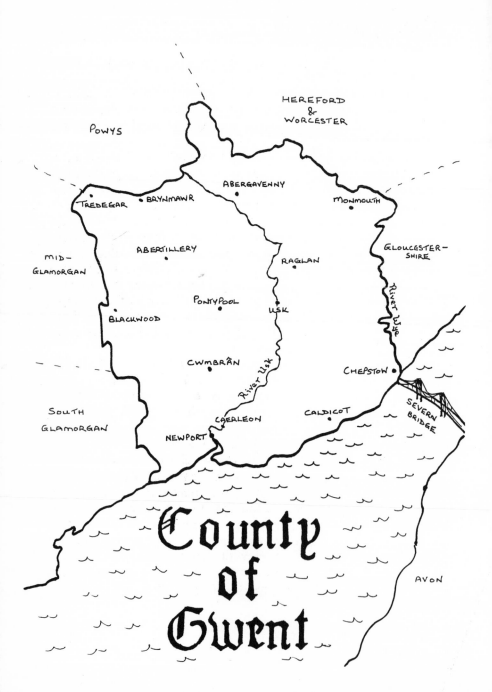

POWYS

HEREFORD
&
WORCESTER

ABERGAVENNY

TREDEGAR • • BRYNMAWR

MONMOUTH •

MID-
GLAMORGAN

ABERTILLERY •

RAGLAN •

GLOUCESTER-
SHIRE

River Wye

BLACKWOOD •

PONTYPOOL •

USK •

CWMBRÂN •

River Usk

CHEPSTOW •

SOUTH
GLAMORGAN

CAERLEON •

CALDICOT •

SEVERN
BRIDGE

NEWPORT •

AVON

County
of
Gwent

Abersychan 🦋

'Aber' means confluence, 'sych' means dry, the name for the stream deriving from its disappearance below ground at times. The Afon Lwyd flows from north to south along the most easterly of the South Wales valleys, a valley whose western slopes have been despoiled by man's search for mineral wealth, while the eastern side remains green and thickly wooded.

Abersychan lies midway between Pontypool and Blaenafon, at the confluence of Nant Sychan with the Afon Lwyd. It grew rapidly in size from the end of the 18th century, when men flocked in from all parts of Britain and from France to seek employment in the ironworks and coal pits. Houses, chapels, pubs and shops soon spread uphill towards the neighbouring villages of Talywaun and Garndiffaith to create a densely populated, busy community. The traditional white farmhouses were surrounded by rows of grey stone cottages and red brick houses. Meanwhile, the mountains became honeycombed with coal levels; furnaces and foundries flourished; tramroads, inclines and railway lines took the riches down to the valley floor and thence away to the south.

Abersychan had its own local Board from the late 1850s, became a civil parish in 1894 and had a greater population than had Pontypool before the creation of the borough of Torfaen amalgamated all the valley authorities. The ecclesiastical parish was created in 1844, a church having already been built at Talywaun as a chapel of the parish of Trevethin.

There were two railway lines, one in the valley bottom and the other at a higher level through Pentwyn, Talywaun and Garndiffaith, both carrying coal from Blaenafon and providing passenger services. Older residents can still remember Abersychan at its busiest, with the many taverns and shops open late into the evening, the chapels packed with people every Sunday and the Co-operative Society hall alive with social activity. The advent of motorised transport and closure of local industry led to depopulation and to the demise of many thriving organisations.

Today, the ever increasing flow of traffic along the A4043 robs what remains of the village street of its former friendly atmosphere.

Nevertheless, a walk round Abersychan is well worthwhile, particularly for those interested in social history. Leave your car in the car park near the site of the former water mill. Stroll up the steep High Street between stone cottages and peep round the corner into Brynteg, where the magnificent facade of the Congregational chapel (1864) faces the former Workmen's Institute, now the public library. Continue uphill, with Trinity chapel on the left opposite to the old Co-operative buildings. Were you to carry on, you would pass two more chapels, High Street Baptist and Noddfa.

Turn right into Factory Lane, so named after the shoe factory which used to occupy the site on the left-hand corner, later to become a theatre and cinema. Walking uphill with a high stone wall to the right, you will come to double gates, through which Glansychan Park is seen. A mansion, property of land and mine owners, stood here but was demolished in 1937.

Turn left into Old Lane (even steeper) as far as the cross-roads, and turn right into Manor Road, formerly called the Dram Road. Created originally as a route for horse-drawn trams laden with coal, its steady winding descent now tests the skill of car, lorry and coach drivers. The comprehensive school and leisure centre lie to the right. A higher elementary school and pupil teachers' centre was built here in 1914, to be replaced in time by grammar and technical schools.

Continue along the road for a few hundred yards until the houses on the left are passed. The steep bank there is part of an incline which replaced the tramroad in taking coal trucks from Talywaun down to join the railroad in the valley. There is pedestrian access to the lower part of the incline, but pause for a moment before descending, to look at the view. On top of the spur of land ahead lies Garndiffaith, with a multitude of assorted houses clinging to the steep slopes down through Victoria village. Out of sight below is Victoria school, built for the growing population in 1903.

Taking the path downhill now, you see ahead the Lasgarn Woods, particularly beautiful in autumn and offering delightful walks. Incline Road then leads direct to the Twyn y Ffrwd Inn, which has stood for centuries on rising ground above the river, while roads and railways have followed changing courses on either side.

To reach the centre of the village, we shall follow the old road, taking a left turn from Ffrwd Road between walls only a few feet apart. Cross the new road with great care. At this point it follows the former railway line. Bear right, the road dipping towards the Afon Lwyd where trees overhang and the noise of traffic is left behind. In earlier days, the gas-works and many houses crowded the further bank while trains rattled along the line above and the narrow road was alive with people. New flats and houses now afford more comfortable living. Turn right at the end, then left along the last part of Old Road, rising to join the main road opposite the former police station, to the left of which is the old lock-up.

Beaufort 🐚

The village of Beaufort owes its origin to the coming of the ironworks in 1780. Before that it was just a hamlet, the area densely wooded, swampy and thinly populated. The few settlements were small, widely separated groups of stone huts on the high ground, linked to each other by tracks along the ridges.

In 1922, 13 bronze axe heads dating back to 500 BC were found beneath a flat stone slab. The soil above the axe heads was not rich, but that which lay below was. Coal, iron ore and limestone were easily obtained as they often appeared together on the surface and this attracted the English ironmasters to the area. One of these was Edward Kendall who built the first blast furnace on the banks of the Ebbwy river at Glanyrafon. The area was called Cendl, the Welsh name for Kendall. Cottages were built for the workers and some old street names still exist, namely Yard Row and Furnace Street.

In the 18th century the land passed to the Duke of Beaufort from his ancestors, the Earls of Worcester, who lived at Raglan Castle, and so Cendl became Beaufort.

Beaufort is well situated, within easy reach of large towns in England and Wales. It consists of a main road roughly a mile long, along which were built its chapels, churches and public houses. Beaufort has no outstanding architectural buildings but the Seven Arches at the bottom of Beaufort, carrying the main railway line, were worthy of mention. These were demolished when the railway closed.

A love of singing has always existed here; chapel and church choirs, male voice and chorals. Many of these – particularly male choirs – have travelled far from Beaufort to give pleasure to thousands. Carmel chapel was the venue for many 'grand concerts', attended by well known singers and pianists. Madam Clara Novello-Davies, mother of Ivor Novello, played there.

Beaufort also had a cinema, built more than 70 years ago, which is now the Municipal Theatre, while below it is Beaufort Ballroom which started as a billiard hall. Opposite the cinema was the railway station, linking Beaufort with all stations to Cardiff. Now, green lawns and flower beds have taken the place of steam trains and platforms, and on this green area grow the three trees planted by Beaufort WI on 8th November 1990.

Blaina 🌿

The villages of Blaina and Nantyglo are situated between two mountains in the valley which was known in the past as the Western Valley. The town to the north of them is Brynmawr and to the south is Abertillery. They owe their existence to the industrial revolution which brought ironmasters to the area. Coalbrookvale – virtually an English translation of Nantyglo – was so named when the ironmaster George Brewer came and built the Coalbrookvale ironworks.

Coalbrookvale House was built by him as his personal residence and was, at the time, one of the finest houses within this community. Built circa 1820, it was noted for the fact that it was the first local house to have a lavatory with running water! George Brewer was one of the few ironmasters who refused to employ children under ten years of age. Over the past century the house has fallen further and further into decay. Half the house was demolished in 1974, but the facade of the house is still much the same as 150 years ago, with the original front door.

Within half a mile of the house can be seen the round tower built by Crawshay Bailey, another ironmaster of Nantyglo, to defend himself from his workers. Those were violent times. The mountain behind Coalbrookvale House is the area that was roamed by 'Scotch Cattle'. These were the early trade unionists who met secretly, dressed in cattle skins and who paid visits from time to time to the homes of workers who were not prepared to support the early union formation in the ironworks. Legend has it that on certain nights of the year the ghosts of the 'Scotch Cattle' can be seen still roaming the mountain above Coalbrookvale.

There is an iron bridge in 'Exeter' which was built in Blaina ironworks in 1834 and up to the present day is still being used. In the middle of the 19th century the iron industry started to decline. Between 1861 and 1871 there was great poverty and the population fell because many people left the district and went to the United States of America, to look for new jobs. In 1880, however, coal was in great demand to satisfy the steam-powered ships of the world's navies, consequently more mines had to be opened. The valley from Blaina to Risca was dotted with coal mines.

All the mines in Blaina are now closed. There is not much industry in Blaina today, though there is an industrial estate on the Rising Sun site consisting of a couple of factories. A lot of people go out of town for employment.

Blaina has produced several good male singers over the years. One was Arthur Fear, a baritone, who in 1932 had the honour of being selected to sing the lead part in the opera *Casanova* at the London Coliseum.

Blaina had a lovely church, St Peter's, but sadly it had to be taken down as it was unsafe. It had a beautiful steeple which was a landmark. Another church was built in its place, but it is of course a modern building. The only other large building in Blaina is the Institute which is now used for most of the events that go on in the community, such as evening classes, dances, clubs and snooker. It also houses the local library. It was built in 1893, the miners contributing a little each week out of their wages towards the cost. In March 1993 the centenary was celebrated with a week of entertainment – concerts, dancing, something different each night.

The Bryn ✣

There are many Bryns in Wales, for the name means bank or hill, but this one is a small village a few miles south east of Abergavenny in the heart of the parish of Llangattock-nigh-Usk, or Llangattock-juxta-Usk as it was sometimes called. At the turn of the century, the Bryn was a small attractive village made up of a few houses and a cluster of whitewashed cottages built on what was at one time the bank of the river Usk.

The church, which is at the far end of the village, is dedicated to St Cadoc and was built on what was the river bank but now, like the village of the Bryn, is separated from the river by a large meadow and so is about 500 yards from the water. There are not only some very interesting memorial stones in the church and churchyard but remains of a late medieval cross stand beyond the north side of the church and opposite the entrance porch is a rare example of a 'kneeling-stone'.

The Old Rectory is next to the church and its present occupier says that there is a friendly ghost in residence. In the 1860s, Penpergwm House, which is now a private nursing home, was built as the new rectory and the first rector to live there was the Rev Corfield. Dr Horace Corner was the last rector to reside in the village as it then became linked with other parishes. Dr Corner's main mode of transport around the parish was a motor-bike and sidecar.

The land surrounding the village is attached to Rectory Farm and has been farmed by the same family for several generations.

The village has changed considerably over the years. Old cottages (some of the first in the village) stood in the lane which is now the driveway of Glandwr. These cottages had a thatched roof which was later replaced by corrugated tin. After Glandwr was built the cottages became derelict and when the Gunter family moved there in the late 1960s they used the remaining stones to build a retaining wall at the bottom of the garden.

River View was occupied by Mrs Alexander who proudly displayed, on the wall of her front room, a Proficiency Certificate of Midwifery. It is said that she was a marvellous midwife who never lost a baby. Mrs Alexander was highly thought of as far away as Llanover and lived to the age of 88 years.

The post office was, at one time, separate from the village store and was run by Mrs Barton. During the 1950s the post office was relocated to opposite the school, into the building which was first the village store. During the Second World War, Mr Alistair Watkins recalls, he was taken prisoner and after living on black bread and olives he used to dream of the village shop and the tall glass jars in which his favourite sweets as a child (coloured sugar-coated fish) were kept. Fortunately the village still retains the amenity of a post office and store and the children still go there for their sweets.

The parish was very lucky to have Mr Leslie Pym MP for Monmouth living at Penpergwm Lodge. He was residing there during the war years and at the time of the Silver Jubilee in 1935, and the Coronation in 1937.

In 1937 four cottages were built in the field of Pentwyn and were named Coronation Cottages. The field on which these cottages stand belonged to the small farm of Bryn Celyn. The whole of that farmland has now been built on and the house of Bryn Celyn just has a small garden.

The centenary of Llangattock-nigh-Usk school was held in 1976. Many of the parents made period costumes for their children who gave a display of Welsh country dancing. Mr John

Llewelyn, a local solicitor, of the old Penpergwm House (now demolished to make way for the Abergavenny–Raglan dual carriageway) made a large '100' cake.

One of the oldest inhabitants of the Bryn, Mr Percy Drew, attended the celebrations. He was an old pupil of the school; his mother and his wife both taught at the school, his mother being headmistress for a time. Another past pupil, Miss Judy Jenkins was headmistress of the school at the time of the celebrations. To mark the day's events each pupil was given a Welsh love spoon as a memento. Sadly, in 1993 the school closed, a great loss to the village.

In 1977 the new village hall was opened. This replaced the old wooden 'hut' (as it was known) with its antiquated kitchen and outside loo. Now there is a thriving social club which opens four nights a week and provides a meeting and recreational centre for the community.

Bryngwyn

The parish of Bryngwyn is situated two miles north west of Raglan on the road from Monmouth to Abergavenny. It includes the village of Great Oak but Bryngwyn itself can scarcely be called a village as it consists of scattered farmhouses, dwellings for agricultural and estate workers and private houses. There is also a church, a parish hall and a 'local' inn.

Bryngwyn means 'white hill'. At the focal point of the parish is the church of St Peter, an ancient building of stone, originally in the Early English style of the 13th century. Situated in a field in sight of the church is St Peter's Well. By the main gate at the entrance to the churchyard is a mounting stone of four steps recalling the days when folk rode to church on horseback and would use the stone to remount their horses.

Until 1979 residents in Bryngwyn, were able to claim that the local general post office was undisputably and officially the smallest post office in the British Isles. It was frequently visited by curious visitors and photographers. All business was transacted through a window three feet by one and a quarter feet, and it had been owned and managed by the same family since 9th June 1898.

Poem of Bryngwyn People

1. We're nobody particular
We're just the men you meet
At harvest with sickle, or
At seedtime dropping wheat
From Mondays until Saturdays
We work from morn till night,
And only in these latter days
We've learnt to read and write.

2. Our little place is poor enough
Though clean as any pin
Who e'er you are, you're sure enough
Of welcome when you're in
The rich man has his valets, and
His locks to guard his store;
But we have empty wallets, and
We only latch the door.

3. Besides, perhaps, a pair or two
Of blankets and a bed,
An Oaken Chest, a chair or two —
All bought when we were wed —
There's little you would lend upon
We've neither house or lands
We only depend upon
The labour of our hands.

4. When these begin to fail you, and
You're thrown upon yourself,
Or anything should ail you and,
there's nothing on the shelf,
Though anxious looks the Moth, and
Our own is almost bare
We feel for one another and,
We find a bit to spare.

5. You ask me what we think about
In raining weather, when
We sit and pass the drink about
And speak but now and then,
Sure all may spend their leisure in
The manner that they will
And poor men find a pleasure
Just simply sitting still.

6. We're up to tend the cattle, when
The Londoner's in bed;
We hear the thunder rattle, when
There's nothing overhead
To shield us in the racket, and
When down doth pour the rain
We only shake our jacket, and
We go to work again.

7. Our daughters serve for wages, and
Our boys go on the farm
According to their ages, and
The Power that keeps from harm.
The sparrows and the likes with
Their glory doth array
Our hearts doth know, and still is with
Our little ones away.

8. To every man his station, and
His work is set I ween:
The Queen doth rule the nation, and
The soldier guards the Queen
From the men that would harm her, and
Their number is not small
We labour for the farmer, and
The Farmer keep them all.

9. Then, do not judge us blindly, as
You'll hear some people do;
Think only of us kindly, as
You'd have us think of you;
To other folk than we belong
The pulpit and the pew,
But England were not England long
Without her common men.

Richard Crawley   1879

The Buckholt

The ancient hamlet of the Buckholt lies two miles from the town of Monmouth on the old Hereford Road (A466) and extends to the county boundary of Herefordshire. The scattered residences are mainly a ribbon development along the roadside or straddling the Mally brook which runs between the counties and forms a somewhat dark valley in places as one proceeds northward.

The name Buckholt means 'beech wood'. An early reference to beeches in the Buckholt is made in a survey of the manor of Monmouth in the year 1560. The Buckholt wood, about 175 acres in extent, is historically the most interesting part of the district. Its importance was recognised in a charter drawn up as early as 1248 by John de Monmouth granting certain rights and privileges to the monks at Monmouth Priory, who owned the property at that time. In 1682 the wood and its surrounding land

Cottages at The Buckholt

came into the possession of the newly created Duke of Beaufort and remained with that family until recent years when it was sold and is now handled by a Forestry Management Company.

The Buckholt wood covers many acres at the northern end and smaller woods fringe the eastern boundary. Between these woods, rising abruptly at the mouth of the valley below the Buckholt Old Mill Farm, where monks came in medieval days to grind their corn, is a small mound called Grist Castle Hill. From its dominating position it was possibly fortified at one time, acting as a defence outpost to guard the road from Monmouth to Hereford as it runs northward through the narrow valley.

Most of the cottages in the Buckholt were built in the 18th and 19th centuries and had their roofs and lintels constructed of round poles from the wood, the stone being produced by the Buckholt quarry. Several cottages were built in the wood, including one known locally as 'murder cottage' because of a murder which was committed there in the 1820s. These were mainly occupied by charcoal burners, but have in this generation fallen into decay. Charcoal burning was carried out in the Buckholt woods for at least 800 years but this ceased in about 1890. Making the piles of wood for the wood-burning was a complicated and skilful job. The completed pile was about the size of a small room and was covered over with earth to exclude air. The burning wood must only smoulder – if flames broke out that part of the timber was spoilt. There is a splendid Neolithic camp right in the middle of the wood and every type of Bronze Age and Roman weapon and pot has been found there.

Notable buildings in the village include St John's church which celebrated its centenary in 1989. Before this church was completed services took place in the little church school at St John's house opposite. The school was built in the 1860s and was in use for 40 years – about 29 children went to school there. The Old Inn at Manson Cross was built in 1760 and was often used by highwaymen. The initials 'PE' over the door stand for Philip Endale who built it. The Plough Inn at Buckholt was used by the charcoal burners and millers but both inns are now private residences.

It seems likely that the Buckholt mill, now a farm, is the most ancient building in the hamlet, being mentioned as 'my new mill of the Buckholt' by Lord John de Monmouth in his 1248 charter. This mill continued to grind corn for over 600 years until the end of the 19th century.

The Buckholt village hall at Manson Cross was built in 1929 by public subscription. It has been the centre of all village activities over the years and housed events such as the annual flower show, the Dramatic Society, the Village Produce Association, the youth club, the weekly Olde Tyme Dance Club, the village fete, the Women's Institute, the Mothers' Union, the mother and toddler group and the table tennis club. In 1960 the village fete was opened by the Duchess of Beaufort who was pleased to attend because of her family's long association with the Buckholt.

Today there is a thriving retirement club which has its home at the hall, and a drama group which performs stage plays and also takes them to other villages so that they too may enjoy them. A gymkhana is held annually. The hall committee arranges village and musical evenings as well as coffee evenings to maintain the hall for future generations.

The village still has a local inn, The Royal Oak on the main road one mile from Monmouth. The post office and shop closed in 1981.

Every year until 1984 the children of the Buckholt were given a Christmas party in the hall and each received a gift from the Christmas tree. Until 1962 the senior citizens also had a Christmas party but since then, instead, they have been taken on an annual summer outing and provided with a three course meal.

The Welsh Water Board has treatment plants at the northern extremity of the Buckholt and these deal with water from a spring which rises in the Buckholt wood and supplies Monmouth as well as the Buckholt.

The Buckholt quarry is still operational and provided the stone for Monmouth Haberdasher's schools and more recently produced over 1,000 tons to restore the old town wall at Hereford following the Tesco development there.

In the old days people worked locally on farms or in residential domestic service – since the 1950s they have also been employed in local shops and offices. They walked or cycled to work and children thought nothing of walking the two miles to school and back. Today many of the people living in the Buckholt are retired but nearly every family has a car and some of the younger people commute daily to Chepstow, Newport and Cardiff.

Caerleon 🐾

Caerleon is an ancient town-village, or village-in-a-town, four miles from Newport. It has a long, long history.

Many people come to this famous little place to see the remains of the fortress of the Second Augustan Legion of the army of ancient Rome. They explore what is left of the legionary baths, the amphitheatre, the defensive wall and turrets, the barracks,

Roman Ampitheatre at Caerleon

ovens and latrine, and they visit the splendid museum, a branch of the National Museum of Wales.

Older even than Roman Britain is the great Iron Age hillfort of Belinstoke on Lodge Hill, high above the Usk valley and the houses. Its great banks and ditches, tree-clad and bracken-covered, are a place of beauty and most impressive. Southward, on a clear day, you may glimpse the shimmering waters of the Severn estuary, and the far shore and hills of that foreign country, England! Northward the green sheep-dappled meadows of Gwent lead the eye to the distant hills of Abergavenny.

During much of the year it is common to see rows of coaches lined up near the amphitheatre. They bring cohorts of school-children. In the splendid museum they thrill to the sight of life-sized and lifelike figures of Roman soldiers, and the lavish display of the life-style of Isca legionary fortress, nearly 2,000 years ago. They, and older people also, gaze in wonder at the scatter of minutely engraved semi-precious stones, lost (and found) in the drains of the baths; and at the broken neck of a Roman amphora, all the way from Rhodes in the eastern Mediterranean, with 'LEG II AVG' painted on it. And what sort of a man was Julius Valens, veteran of the Legion who, his memorial stone tells us, lived to the age of 100. What tales he could have told (and probably did) of life with the Eagles!

During the summer school holidays a site adjacent to the museum is busy with children learning how to make pottery, cook and dress in ancient Roman fashion. What a wonderful way to learn history.

The story of Caerleon, Roman Isca, did not cease when the Second Legion marched away for the last time. There are legends of King Arthur and his Knights: the green hollow of the amphi-theatre before its excavation was known to local folk as King Arthur's Round Table. After 1066 came the Normans. Their mound or motte between the Roman defences and the river is one of many in these parts. Perhaps it is inevitable that it has attracted Arthurian legend. We are assured that the king built a tall tower on the top of it, so that Guinevere could see Somerset!

From many viewpoints in the lower Usk valley the lovely tower of St Cadoc's church can be seen rising above the trees. Caerleon is one of the most venerable homes of Christianity in Britain. In Roman times, in the mid 2nd century, according to Geoffrey of Monmouth it became a bishopric; one of three with London and York. And it was probably at Caerleon that St Julian and St Aaron were martyred in about AD 279.

The present church, which stands on the site of the Roman headquarters, incorporates remains of the former Norman church, and the tower dates partly from the 12th or 13th century. Its fine peal of eight bells gives a glorious sound.

Caerleon still possesses some fine old inns. Ancient and pictur-esque are The Old Bull, The Hanbury Arms, The Red Lion, the

Priory Hotel, The Ship and The Bell in the 'village' beyond the bridge. Tennyson stayed at The Hanbury Arms when he was writing *Idylls of the King*. The old tower at The Hanbury Arms, partially built of Roman stones, was probably part of the medieval castle defences.

Charles Williams is a name unlikely to be forgotten in Caerleon. In the 17th century he fought a duel with a cousin, and killed him. He fled abroad, prospered, and eventually returned to England, dying in 1720. In his will he left a legacy to his native town, school and church. The old school building bears a commemorative plaque, and is still used as part of the modern school, which continues to benefit generously from Charles's legacy. St Cadoc's church is adorned with a fine series of stained glass windows in his memory.

From Roman times onward Caerleon was a port, down to the Industrial Revolution, when an iron and coal tramroad led down to a quay by the bridge. All that has now gone: there is a 'New Port' downriver.

In these ever-changing times, modern residential estates have been built on the outskirts of the village; but the old village High Street, which follows the line of one of the main streets of the Roman fortress, is as sleepy as modern motor traffic will allow it to be. There you can still be greeted with a friendly 'good morning' or enjoy a leisurely chat with a fellow Caerleonite, in true and enduring village tradition.

Caldicot ✤

Caldicot is situated five miles south west of Chepstow, bounded by the river Severn to the south and the M4 to the north. It will acquire a very prominent western boundary on the completion of an access road from the M4 to the second Severn crossing.

There are two interpretations of its name: either a corruption of 'Cil-y-coed' meaning skirt of the wood, which is difficult to understand now that so many trees have disappeared under concrete; or 'Cold cot', a rough shelter built by the Romans on a main road to provide a haven for travellers. This second meaning is the most likely because the Roman town of Caerwent is just two miles to the north and the Roman garrison town of Caerleon only ten miles away.

In 1086, Caldicot was held under Sheriff Durand and was recorded in the Domesday Book as being 'in demesne, three ploughs and 15 villeins, four serfs and one man at arms. All these have twelve ploughs. Here is a mill of ten shillings. All is worth £6.'

The population of Caldicot has risen significantly over the past 150 years. The building and opening of the railway from Swansea to Chepstow, the Severn Tunnel and the marshalling yards swelled the population between 1850 and 1900. Workers and their families came mainly from the West Country and the North of England, bringing with them everything to sustain a growing and thriving community.

Caldicot remained very English in outlook but when Llanwern steelworks came into operation in 1958 things changed. Workers and their families still came from the North, but the valleys of South Wales and especially Ebbw Vale provided a large workforce. The Welsh accent is now dominant on the streets of Caldicot but just occasionally the Gloucestershire 'burr' can be heard.

Many of those Welsh voices are now to be heard in the male voice choir, which has an international reputation. The silver band, the football club, students of the comprehensive school and the choir make regular exchanges with the twin town of Waghausel, Germany. The Women's Institute was struggling but active with just six members in 1979. They were determined not to let it die and now it is thriving. They involve themselves with local issues, for example the St David's Foundation, an organisation started in Newport for the care and support of patients and their families coping with terminal illness.

A favourite local walk is the path skirting the castle and through the adjoining 45 acres of country park. The park is a venue for the annual carnival and the very popular May Day spectacular organised by the Chepstow Round Table. It is also a regular campsite for visiting caravan clubs. Medieval banquets are held in the great hall of the castle and taking pride of place within the walls is a cannon from the *Foudroyant*, one of Nelson's flagships. There is much to interest the historian in the area of the medieval castle including the old manor house of Llanthony Secunda and a small 15th century church. Recently an archaeological dig beside the river Nedern revealed Bronze Age relics, taking the record of human activity in the area even further back in time. The Nedern valley is flooded for most of the winter, attracting wildfowl and the famous Bewick swans that fly in from northern Russia.

A certain Henry Jones, purveyor of flour and biscuits in Bristol, lived in Caldicot. In 1846 this Mr Jones invented one of the most significant products of his time; self-raising flour. Within six years he had granted licences to make the flour in the USA, Australia and New Zealand. When Florence Nightingale complained to the *Times* about the sour bread supplied to the troops in the Crimea, Henry Jones took on the Admiralty in her support. Eventually the Army and the Navy were using the new flour. Finally, he was appointed purveyor of patent flour and biscuits to Queen Victoria.

It is a shame that Caldicot has lost many of the qualities of a quiet rural community, hidden from the people travelling from West Wales to the Midlands or eastwards via the ferry at Beachley to cross the Severn. The economic developments of the 19th century that brought the railway to Caldicot have been superseded by the 20th century developments of the second Severn crossing, the proposed new motorway and a potential airport. Parts of Caldicot retain their rural charm, whilst other areas are greatly affected by development and change. It is contrasts such as these which have created the Caldicot which can be seen today and which will ensure its survival as a thriving community in the future.

Catbrook 🐚

Catbrook appears on the map as a rather isolated little hamlet made up of a rambling group of houses far from any town. However, this very isolation has created a warm and friendly village with plenty of life and enthusiasm. It has maintained its own identity without being swallowed up into large estates, and is part of the area of outstanding natural beauty within the Wye valley. It is six miles from Monmouth to the north and from Chepstow to the south.

There have been tremendous changes in the village over the last 50 years. There used to be a post office, grocer, butcher and bakery, but now only a little post office remains. As in many other rural communities the village school was recently closed (1987), and the children are now bussed into Trelleck. The little church survives, however, and is very active. It can proudly boast a Flower Festival which in 1993 raised £800 for church funds.

In the name of 'progress' the village has been forced to change and adapt. It was one of the last villages to receive electric power in the early 1950s, and until that time it had remained a low density, isolated community. The electric power, the Severn Bridge, the M4 and, of course, the explosion in car ownership, have gradually opened up the village, but so far it has largely retained its character and peaceful atmosphere.

Tourism may be perceived as another possible threat to village life but at present few tourists venture away from Tintern to drive up the very narrow, winding lane to Catbrook. The village is part of the Wye valley which is one of the last remaining virgin valleys with undisturbed land on either side.

Croesyceiliog 🐚

Situated on the old main road between Newport and Pontypool (A4042) is Croesyceiliog. Originally part of the manor of Edlogan, this ancient possession of the Welsh lords of Caerleon once belonged to Henry VII and then Henry VIII and was purchased from the Crown in 1558 by William Morgan of Pontypool, eventually passing to John Hanbury of Pontypool. The cottages clustered around the Upper Cock Inn became known as Croes-y-Ceiliog – the Cross of the Cock.

In 1949 the area in and around the village was incorporated with the designated site of Cwmbran New Town. Old buildings were demolished willy-nilly but fortunately one or two remain.

Originally the people of Croesyceiliog were farmers and agricultural workers, but the coming of the tin-plate industry attracted new workers and the village grew. With the demise of this industry workers became engaged in light engineering at various factories in the area.

The foundation stone of Pontrhydyrun Baptist church was laid on 13th May 1815 on land given by William Conway, the owner of the tin-plate works, for a chapel for the benefit of his workers and their families. The original building was pulled down in 1836 and at a cost of £2,000 the present chapel was erected and opened for worship on 16th August 1837. After various renovations the chapel buildings were registered as of special historical interest in 1951.

The Upper Cock Inn is a very ancient inn standing at the crossroads of The Garw and The Highway. The inn has been modernised in recent years and the old signs carved on stone are now incorporated on a triangular stone plinth beneath a stained glass lamp. The sign reads:

'Dyma Dafarn Croes y ceiliog
Groesaw I Bob un am ei ceiniog
Cwrw da I bawb trwy dalu
Dewch I mewn chwi gewch ei brofi.

Here is an inn, the cross of the cock
A welcome is yours for a penny
For payment so small a good beer waits you all
Come in, taste our ale, good as any.'

The name of the inn probably derived from the extra horses – 'cock' horses – used to draw loads up the hill.

In 1839 the Eastern Valley contingent of the Chartists, a popular reform movement, marched from Blaenafon to Newport passing through Croesyceiliog and halting at the Upper Cock Inn where they took refreshments, dried their gunpowder in an oven and calling at the nearby cottages, pressed men into their service.

The cottages behind the Upper Cock Inn in Lower Garw Road were completely renovated about 15 years ago and the architect won an award for this project.

Just before the junction of The Highway and Woodland Road there is a small house known as Jim Crow's Cottage. In 1823 this was the home of a gentleman named Benjamin Evans. He was a schoolmaster, postmaster and shopkeeper, all duties carried out in his little house. He and his wife had a very good friend, an English seafarer by the name of Jim Crow and when he died they named their cottage after him.

Croesyceiliog has become the administrative centre of Gwent. The Gwent Police Headquarters and Gwent County Hall are situated on Turnpike Road. The old junior school on The Highway is now the office of the County Probation Community Services and the Gwent crematorium is on the outskirts on the Treherbert Road.

Croesyceiliog comprehensive school is situated on the fields John Lewis, the miller, used to cross on his way to his mill at Llanyrafon.

For as long as The Spout, a spring that never runs dry, keeps flowing in The Garw and the Afon Lwyd, the grey river, still forms the western boundary between the old village and the new town, the people of Croesyceiliog will continue to fight to keep the area our community, even though it is no longer quite our village.

Cross Ash 🐚

In the north east corner of Gwent, Cross Ash lies on the B4521 Ross-on-Wye to Abergavenny road. It nestles under the 1,300 foot Graig Syfyrddin, from the top of which seven counties may be seen on a clear day. It is a beautiful area of scattered dwellings, mixed farming and woodland with abundant wildlife lying between the three castles of Skenfrith, Grosmont and White Castle, which were built for defence between England and Wales, and were held by and for many famous lords. The Norman church of St Mary, chapels, a shop, a post office, a garage, an inn, the village hall and the school are spread over the parish.

The hall was built by the villagers themselves in the 1950s with much effort with pick and shovel, block and tackle, one spade-lugged tractor and whatever help they could give to work or fundraising. Now adjacent to the hall is the new primary and infants school for 210 pupils, recently opened by the county council at a cost of £2,000,000 to replace six Victorian schools and to offer the children more opportunities. Offa's Dyke runs north–south across the parish and the Three Castles walk is an 18½ mile tour, part of which is the Old Coach Road (Brecon to Gloucester) with its milestone of 1778. White Castle has its legend of the Blind Knight who held the castle by challenging his attacker to a duel in a darkened room, and there are other stories of ghostly hauntings.

Cwmavon 🐚

This small village nestles in the valley of the Afon Lwyd in the centre of Gwent – originally called Monmouthshire. One local resident has vivid memories of the past.

'When I first knew it in the late 1920s it had a thriving Wesleyan chapel and a large Sunday school; sadly the chapel has been pulled down and the Sunday school is now the village hall. On the eastern side of the valley lie nine or ten small farms and in the village there were five rows of cottages, as well as about two dozen houses.

We had a railway station from where you could catch trains to Blaenafon, Pontypool and Newport, but alas, no trains now. On one Saturday during the summer all the Sunday schools would travel by train to Barry Island – it was called the 'Blake Outing'.

Cwmavon boasted one small shop at No 5 Forge Row owned by Mr Llewellyn – who was also the Sunday school superintendent. It sold household goods such as soap, scrubbing brushes and blacklead along with sweets, cigarettes and paraffin.

A red horse-drawn van owned by Hynam and Willis the bakers called each day with fresh oven-baked bread – which is rare today. I can remember going out with my mother to tea with a friend of hers and being given my own plate of wafer-thin bread and butter to eat. Thursday was 'ashcart day' when everyone would put out their ashes in buckets to be collected and tipped into the cart, causing quite a dust. It was all taken away by Mr Bladon to be dumped. Fresh milk was delivered to the door daily by Miss Price, whose father farmed Beili-odu Farm; folks would bring out their jugs to be filled from the churn using two measures, either a pint or half pint, which would hang from the neck of the churn when not in use.

Between Varteg and Cwmavon there was a culvert running down the mountain from the Washeries at Varteg, ending up in the Afon Lwyd at the bottom. The men of the village dug 'dobbing ponds' at the edge of this culvert where they would trap the coal dust and when the water drained away they would make 'dobbin balls' which could be used to eke out the coal on the fire – these gave out a good heat but, if poked, would fall away into dust.

There had been a thriving brewery in the village owned by Westlake Breweries, but this lay empty until about 1930 when the Subsistence Production Society took it over to provide work for the men who were unemployed. I don't remember what they made, but they generated their own electricity. The first building to have electric light was the chapel, and soon afterwards my father paid to have our house connected to the electricity supply, so that we had a good light to sew and read by, and gone was the dirty job of cleaning the oil lamps, which were the only other means of light because our village had no gas lamps.

There were two large houses in the village; Cwmavon House which was occupied by Mr Humphries the colliery manager, and the White House in the brewery grounds where the brewery manager had lived, which was empty until taken over as an office for the Production Society. These would have been the only two houses in Cwmavon to have bathrooms and flush toilets; everyone else had tin baths which they used in front of the fire every night, bearing in mind that most of the men were miners. There was no hot water on tap and all water had to be heated on the fire, or in the boilers at the side of the fire.

Looking back life seemed hard, but there were good points. Children could walk the roads, roam the mountainsides and fields and stay out until dark in absolute safety.

I remember my father taking me down to the cricket field at the bottom of the village to watch the local cricket team, of which he was a member, and also a Sunday school picnic in the Barn Field above Prices Farm where we had races, such as egg (made out of china) and spoon and three-legged. Afterwards the grown-ups would boil a kettle on an open fire and we would enjoy a picnic and every child would have a small bag of sweets.

One Saturday in the summer all the Sunday school, parents and children would walk over the mountain, past The Goose and Cuckoo – where you could get a drink of lemonade or a packet of crisps for a penny – to Llanover where we would have a picnic in the park and 'have a go' on the swings before walking home, a trip of eight to nine miles.

Varteg was the nearest school and we all walked up the Snailcreep or the Shop Road to school and back home to lunch; there were no school meals in those days. If the weather was very bad we were allowed to take sandwiches and eat them in school. When I got home I had to change out of my good school clothes and put on a pinafore, then my mother would teach me to darn, patch and knit, or I was allowed to read until bedtime. I had three friends who lived at the bottom of the village in a house belonging to the railway (their father was a stationmaster) and

I spent many happy hours in their big garden where we were allowed to have our own small patch where we grew flowers and played hide and seek in among the trees. Such are my memories of a happy childhood in our valley.'

Inevitably, there have been changes in the last half century, but the village still has much to offer by way of interesting historical walks, beautiful countryside and an inn where excellent refreshments are served.

Cradled between the mountains, Cwmavon retains the tranquil serenity of yesteryear and will prove a satisfying experience for all those seeking respite from the hurlyburly of current daily life.

Cwmyoy & Llanthony

Although most people hereabouts live within the parish of Cwmyoy, and telephone and tax bills arrive addressed Upper or Lower Cwmyoy, it is Llanthony that is the real focus for what is not so much a village but more a community some ten miles long and scarcely a mile wide, scattered the length of the beautiful Vale of Ewyas.

Running south to north through the Black Mountains of Gwent, the valley is confined by two high ridges, the Ffawddog and the Hatterrall; along the latter runs Offa's Dyke Path, and from its heights the walker can peer down into the lush woodlands and sloping meadows of the Vale of Ewyas, or gaze eastward over the gently rolling, rich pasturelands of south Herefordshire. This is the land of the South Wales Marches, where history and legend are almost indistinguishable and every old house and ancient settlement has its share of both.

For the visitor entering from the southern end, the valley proper really starts at the Queen's Head Inn, where the left-hand road rises steeply to the Gaer, an Iron Age fort, and the right-hand turning dips down over the little river Honddu and rises again to the tiny village of Cwmyoy. The village is no more than a cluster of half a dozen houses and a church, clinging precariously to an outcrop of rock which, because of a geological fault, slipped down

Church of St Martin, Cwmyoy

the mountainside some time in the Middle Ages, taking the ancient church with it. This is well worth a visit. Securely buttressed against further slippage, it is clearly twisted and leaning, and the interior view towards the altar is disorientating, to say the least, perhaps suggesting to some visitors that the cider they had with lunch was stronger than they suspected.

None of the village stands on what is now the main road, the B4423. This is a glacial valley and centuries ago the bottom would have been far too wet to build upon. Even on the hills many died of consumption – silent witnesses being the tiny graves in the churchyard. One inscription, on the grave of a mother died aged 34, and her son aged three days, reads:

'The old must die, we are all agree,
Likewise the young, you plainly see.
Therefore prepare, and pray for grace,
For here is no abiding place.'

Back down on the valley road, which demands great caution and patience – be prepared to reverse for tractors and wait for sheep and pony trekkers – and another few miles will bring you to Llanthony itself, with its ruined Norman priory now housing the Abbey Hotel.

The history of this place is really that of the whole Vale of Ewyas and has shaped the world's view of it. It began when St David chose to build himself a hermit's cell here in the 6th century, living – so tradition has it – on water and the wild leeks that later became the national symbol. (Apparently it was the Victorians who replaced them with the daffodil, finding a common vegetable rather undignified.) Even the name Llanthony, by which the valley is now best known, derives from the saint's residence there, being a corruption of Llandewi nant Honddu, or the church of St David on the Honddu brook.

Some 600 years later a Norman knight discovered the place while out hunting and was so affected by its tranquil beauty that he immediately announced his intention of spending the rest of his days there in religious retreat. He re-inhabited the saint's rough hermitage but eventually his powerful kinsmen, the De Lacys, insisted on founding the priory, in its time renowned as one of the most splendid in the realm. Sadly, because of political unrest, it flourished for a mere 30 years, declining steadily until the dissolution in the 16th century.

The priory and its estates, comprising most of the valley, then passed through a succession of owners, one of whom in the 18th century fitted up the south west tower as a shooting lodge, which to this day forms the basis of the hotel. Shortly after this the estate was acquired by Walter Savage Landor, romantic poet and essayist. His attempts to turn it into a gentleman's estate on the English model met with disaster and he was eventually forced to flee abroad to escape his creditors, although he left behind a still appreciable legacy in the form of thousands of tree plantings, including Spanish chestnuts and European larches.

Devauden 🐚

Devauden lies where the St Arvans to Monmouth road rises to the top of the ridge of hills above Chepstow. Possible derivations of the name include a corruption of the Welsh for beech, ffawydden, or perhaps a variation of Diwauden, implying the black lea, a reference to the ancient practice of charcoal burning in the area.

The green still provides a focus for village life and is the site of annual celebrations on 5th November. On the south east side of the green stands the Hood Memorial Hall, a valuable village resource, the land for which was donated by Lady Curre earlier this century. The building was constructed with money given by Mrs Hood and opened for use in 1953. The only public house in the village is The Mason's Arms. This is on the north side of the green, and has stood on this site for nearly 200 years.

Devauden is unusual in having emerged as a village without the central focus of a parish church. There has never been a local squire, only a distant landlord, and the 'local' church for centuries was at Newchurch, three miles away. Consequently, Devauden for many years was more a collection of sturdy, independent folk, working mostly in agriculture and forestry, than a nucleated village community in the usual sense.

The absence of organised religion meant the local people were ripe for the nonconformist teachings of the 18th century. In October 1739 John Wesley preached his first sermon in Wales on the green in Devauden, to a crowd of 300 to 400 people, many of whom had walked miles to hear him. One notable lady, Ann Rosser, having walked to Devauden from Earlswood six miles away, continued to follow Wesley around the county on foot, listening to his teachings and finally returned home to Earlswood to establish one of the first Methodist chapels in Wales.

Nonconformity seems to have flourished in Devauden and its growth may have contributed to the determination of the remarkable James Davies to found first an Anglican school and then a church in the village. The school, where James Davies ate, slept and worked, opened on 15th June 1815. It was financed by the diocese of Llandaff and there Davies educated between 80 and 100 of 'the rude, ragged boisterous mountain children' of Devauden. Davies had a reputation as a strong disciplinarian and is said to have hoisted naughty children up to the rafters in a basket. He never earned more than £20 a year, sometimes less than £15, but despite his own poverty worked tirelessly to relieve the sufferings of others. What is more, he used his own money to refurbish the schoolroom, thereby enabling it to be licensed for divine worship in 1829. In 1830 a new schoolroom was built beside the original building and in June 1836 his dream was realised and the old school was consecrated as a chapel of ease within the parish of Newchurch. In 1848 at the age of 83, this remarkable man left Devauden to start a school at Llangattock Lingoed, where he died, universally loved and revered, in 1849.

Today the church is still in regular use. It is now served by the same vicar as St Arvans, Itton, Penterry and Kilgwrrwg, a grouping which reflects the longstanding historical links between the villages. The village has grown considerably in recent years and building is still in progress. The population is now larger, more mobile and more varied as to occupation and life-style. Despite the population growth, the old school was closed in 1986 and the local children are now bussed to the new school at Shirenewton, a move of which one feels James Davies would not have approved.

Dingestow 🐚

Dingestow is named after the founder of the church, St Dingat, one of the sons of Brychan Brychaniog of Brecon. St Dingat is amongst the least known of the many Celtic saints who have had connections with Gwent. Tradition has it that Dingat was a pupil in a monastic college in Mid Glamorgan, and it was then he established the church at Dingestow. He died locally and was buried here.

The whole church was restored in 1887, the tower having

been almost completely rebuilt in 1847 with five bells. The list of incumbents goes back to 1390, and just a few will remember seven vicars dating from 1928 to the present. For many years Dingestow was twinned with the adjoining parish of Wonastow, but times have changed and the present vicar has five churches to administer.

The remains of Dingestow Castle lie in a field near the road only a hundred yards or so west of the church. It now consists merely of a large mound. The original castle was a wooden fortress, built by the English and demolished by the Welsh at least twice due to the long running territorial dispute. The castle in the true sense was built in 1184, again being attacked by the Welsh. It was finally demolished, having fallen into extreme disrepair, and the stone, it is said, was used for the foundations of local highways.

It was a sad day when the last train travelled the line through Dingestow station. In years gone by everything was delivered by rail, even cattle were brought to the farms by goods train, and one could always judge the time when the whistle blew as the train pulled into the station.

Dingestow Court is a place of historic beauty, which has been in the Bosanquet family since 1801. The late Archbishop of Canterbury, William Temple, was a brother-in-law of the late Sir Ronald Bosanquet, and he often visited Dingestow and preached in the church. He also joined in parties given at the Court at Christmas time for the indoor and outdoor staff.

The Bridge Farm in the centre of the village was originally a coaching inn, where people stayed to rest and change their horses. A rough dirt track ran from Dingestow through Wonastow to Monmouth, the only road then to get to the town. The road got its name 'Jingle Street' because of the jingling of the bells on the horses' harness as they travelled over the rough ground. The Bridge Farm also incorporated the parish room, used for Sunday school, meetings, whist drives etc until the construction of a well built village hall paid for by local farmers on land donated by the Bosanquet family. After being a dairy farm for many years, 'The Bridge' is now a popular and very pleasant caravan park which has brought quite a bit of life to the village.

Due to a new housing development in 1953, 24 council houses and four bungalows were built. Queen's Hill was chosen for the name of the new estate, mostly occupied by farm workers and factory workers at British Nylon at Mamhilad and the Glascoed ammunition works. This development brought electricity and water to the village, a real godsend to those who had struggled so long without these conveniences. It was goodbye then to filling oil lamps, milking by the light of a Tilley lantern and going to bed with a candle, and to carrying water from a nearby spring.

Later on more houses started to appear and soon Charles Road was completed with 32 houses. More recently a private estate has been developed with 21 dwellings, named Tybrith, chosen because they are built adjacent to a very old barn and fields of that name. A private bungalow at the bottom of the estate now brings the total to 82 houses in the village, so Dingestow has grown considerably over the years. Many of the residents are now retired, but there are also quite a number of young families.

Dingestow has a post office and general stores, and a modernised village hall, where each week a keep fit class is held, also a Diamond Club for the over sixties. The Sunday school under their new name, The Seekers meets every Friday, followed by a well run youth club. The Women's Institute meets there too, and a local private school uses it frequently. The hall is hired for many other functions, and is a useful community centre for the villagers and people from surrounding areas. A very popular and newly formed ladies' group named The Link meets monthly at the vicarage too. A team of bellringers practise their skill every week on the six bells which are now in the tower, and an enthusiastic choir leads the singing at the services, so it must be agreed that there aren't many dull moments in life in the country at Dingestow.

Fleur-de-lis

Why Fleur-de-lis – a French name – in a Welsh mining valley? Several explanations are given of its origin. The most popular one seems to be that, because of religious persecution, French

Huguenots left their country and settled in this area. They set up a spelter works and a brewery, thus bringing employment. Locals still refer to it as 'The Flower'. Some say Trelyn was the original name.

This small colliery village, on the east bank of the Rhymney river and about 15 miles from Newport, is bounded by the small hamlet of Gellihaf and also Pengam which were both dependent on Fleur-de-lis for their post office and some small shops. Today, however, most people shop in Bargoed or Blackwood – the two nearest small towns – when not using the out-of-town supermarkets now available.

Until 1878 High Street was a tramway with only the Trelyn Hotel (now demolished), a post office, and Salem chapel. Later, as more shops were built, there were four butcher's shops. The names of the owners made an interesting sentence – Tapper, Herd, Davies, Crow! The only chemist did not always have the required medication in stock so was known as 'Willie-something-similar'. Most of us survived to a ripe old age anyway! The local doctor who did his rounds on horseback had a runner in the Grand National named *Brown Jack*.

The collieries brought immigrants from the English border counties, descendants of whom still live in the village. Today, the immigrants still come because of the new roads. This 'dormitory' village is within easy reach of the new corridor along the motor-ways and is, therefore, very convenient for work and leisure pursuits.

St Luke's church, originally on Gellihaf Road, was the fore-runner of the present St David's church now approaching its centenary. Several of the past vicars are remembered with affection, as were their wives who played an active part in village life. The church was the centre of activity where, in addition to all the usual church functions, several high-class operas were produced. There has always been much talent here, especially in music. The silver band competed at Crystal Palace amongst other engagements. There were six or more other places of worship. All had good Sunday attendances especially when the annual Barry outing was approaching!

On Whit Mondays, the Whitsun March was a grand event with banners flying and much competition amongst all denominations for the loudest singing, which only ceased as chapel passed chapel in close proximity as the procession turned either at Pengam post office (now closed) or 'Flower Square'. After the tea and 'tramline' cake (plain cake sandwiched with jam and cream – only seen on Whit Monday) everyone joined in the fun on the Ynys field. Although the church had its own field, it was not unknown for some to climb through the fence and join the better fun on the Ynys. 'Kiss-in-the-ring' was especially popular. Many a couple met their destiny on the Ynys field – in spite of the clouds of coal dust – by the end of the evening.

There were two collieries, Britannia and Pengam, both now closed. The days of coal dust on everything – the washing, flowers in the garden, picnics and other outdoor activities – are now long gone. The river has been restocked with fish and the fields are green again. The reclaimed coal tips and slag heaps have been planted with trees and shrubs. Many small factory units have been set up providing jobs, especially for women.

The Miners' Institute housed the library, billiard hall and youth club and was host to many wartime concerts – Sybil Thorndyke amongst the variety of stars at the time. The new community centre now provides another meeting place, as does the rugby club.

There are now three schools in the area, in one of which the children are taught through the medium of Welsh. There are few Welsh speakers but many Welsh learners as the language becomes more popular.

When the Women's Institute was formed in 1967 with 100 members plus a waiting list, there was much interest aroused by this organisation new to the area. On the first Tuesday in each month there was not a man to be seen in Fleur-de-lis before 9.30 in the evening. They were all baby-sitting!

Gilwern

The name Gilwern means 'recess of march or alder'. Gilwern village is situated in the Usk valley at the confluence of the rivers Usk and Clydach, and is the gateway to the scenically beautiful Clydach Gorge.

On the hillside above the village commanding a magnificent view of the Vale of Usk stands Llanelly church, dedicated to St Elli. It has served the community since approximately 1150. It was built during the erection of the castles in the surrounding area and contains many features of historical significance. Surrounding the church were 16 yew trees in a circle, made famous by the bowmen of Gwent who used the branches for their bows. Many are still standing and are now hollow.

Gilwern

The cross in the churchyard was regarded as the most sacred spot and everyone wished to be buried near it. In fact at a time when few people could afford a separate memorial stone the cross served as such for everyone. The font is the oldest object in the church, quite plain and bulging at four corners. The oak screen leads to the bell tower with bells inscribed thus: 1440 'Holy Jesu, ever keep this bell sound for thee' (in Latin); 1626 'Fear God, Honour the King'; 1626 'Give Thanks to God'; 1715 the names of the church-wardens; 1908 'Gloria Deo'. One former bellringer by the name of Williams, late of Ty Isha Farm, became the chief ringer at St Paul's cathedral.

The church registers make interesting reading. The first record in 1701 has the name only in Latin. One entry in 1815 is the baptism of Sir Bartle Frere, born in Clydach House. He became a diplomat and was High Commissioner for South Africa. He is buried in the crypt in St Paul's cathedral, London. There is also the entry of baptism of Francis John Jayne, 1845–1921, who became Bishop of Chester. He was the eldest son of John Jayne of Pantybeilau.

In recent years a church centre has been dedicated in the heart of the village. This is used for religious and social gatherings and the new rectory adjoins it.

Prior to 1796, Gilwern village was mainly a farming community although iron was produced in small quantities in Clydach. With the introduction of the use of coal for smelting iron at the Clydach ironworks larger quantities were produced and transportation became a priority. Many tramroads were authorised by Acts of Parliament to serve a canal system. Gilwern became the intersection of the horse-drawn tramroads and canal, linking ironworks, mines, quarries and foundries by canal to Brecon and Newport.

In 1796 work commenced on the construction of the Brecknock and Abergavenny Canal. A commemorative plaque, erected on the canal bank near the Bridge and Navigation Hotel indicates the exact spot where work began. The construction of the canal was an outstanding feat of engineering by hundreds of 'navvies' toiling to build an earthen aqueduct 92 feet high over a large stone culvert or tunnel with a span of 22 feet by 270 feet through which the river Clydach flowed. On completion of the aqueduct the newly constructed wharf became a centre for industry. For nearly 100 years the canal was used for the transportation of iron, limestone, coal, general farm merchandise and livestock. A watercourse from the river took water to provide power to the wheels and turbines of the one-time woollen mill down the valley at Danybont.

Local conditions were quite hard in those days as the writings of Evan James, aged nine in 1841, record. 'I worked in the forges rising the balling furnace door. I am called a "pull-up boy". I work from six to six at night every other week. I get time to eat my dinner when we are working "large orders" but when we are working "small orders" the work is very busy and we have scarcely any time to eat until the end of the turn. I work under the men and get four shillings per week. I have my health very well. I have not lost any time for six months past. I have been in the National school and go to the Sunday school. I can read a little.'

Throughout the area there are interesting houses, the mill, and particularly farm buildings dating from the 17th century onwards, which have a distinct link with the history of the area. One of the larger houses, Ty Mawr (Big House) and estate, has links with the Crawshay family, the ironmakers. Glaslyn, Aberclydach and Pantybeileau are still occupied today.

Over the years the importance of the canal gave rise to a steady increase in the population of the village. Then the coming of the steelworks in Ebbw Vale in the 1930s made Gilwern a desirable and convenient place to live. Houses, shops, churches, schools and public houses were built. Since the Second World War the population has risen to 3,000 plus. The working life of the canal lasted over 90 years and was replaced by a railway.

The railway provided a speedier means of communication over a much larger area of the country. In turn, the railway was replaced by new road facilities, especially the Heads of the Valley Road which links to the M4 and M5 motorways.

The village hall, situated in the centre of the village, was built as a result of local subscriptions. Today the village of Gilwern, whose historical past is steeped in the Industrial Revolution, has returned to its peaceful rural origins in the heart of the Brecon National park.

Goldcliff & Whitson ஜ௸

History at Goldcliff stretches back to at least 12000 BC. An archaeological team from St David's University College, Lampeter has been surveying the foreshore when the tide goes out and has discovered remains from various periods in the past. First are fossilised animal bones from the last glaciation, remains of bison and wolf. Then in 5000 BC people were making tools from flint; the team has found the waste left behind and a spread of charcoal stretching over a wide area, where ancient people burnt down the trees that were growing over the levels at that time. Sea level was a lot lower than it is today.

Later, in the Bronze Age, people were using the levels for hunting and fishing; part of a sewn boat dated by radiocarbon to 1300 BC was found in 1992. The planks had been reused as a platform in the marsh. The most exciting discoveries, however, relate to the Iron Age. Remains of seven rectangular houses about seven by five metres have been discovered. The walls were made of alder timbers, beautifully pointed using an axe. Inside, two large posts held up the roof, probably of reed thatch. Each house had a small doorway on the landward side and trackways led from the houses towards the river. These houses are particularly interesting because they are rectangular. All other British Iron Age houses (and thousands have been excavated) are round.

Conditions on the intertidal area are muddy and can be extremely dangerous. It is not recommended that anyone go out without people to guide them who know the area well.

In the following centuries, many sailors sailed the river Severn, seeing cliffs of golden red sandstone with golden, glittering particles of mica amongst it. Hence the name Goldcliff originated.

A Norman lord called Robert de Chandos (buried in Goldcliff

churchyard) founded Goldcliff Priory, now Hill Farm, in the 12th century. The priory was dedicated to St Mary Magdalene. It was a dependent priory of the Norman abbey of Bec-Hellouin, with a French prior. The monks of the priory had the special privilege of wearing white habits, unlike the traditional black habits worn by Benedictine monks.

The priory was the richest in Wales, and it was believed that the reason for its wealth could be found in a hole in the sea wall leading to the priory, suggesting that the monks benefited from shipwrecks, as did some clergy and many other people from the surrounding area. Wine, tobacco and brandy were the favourite contraband.

The monks built a fresh water pill, Monksditch, to drain the surrounding land, which is below sea level. It runs from Langstone to meet the Severn at Goldcliff. The monks also built Goldcliff salmon fisheries, which is why many say the priory was built 'on the hill' for the monks' Friday fish feasts.

The salmon season runs from March until August, and locals still use baskets called putchers which once were made of withy but are now made of aluminium. At Goldcliff there are two walls of putchers, each four putchers high, one containing 1,000 baskets, the other 900. Now there are also many fishermen who stand on the sea wall rod-fishing. There have been many sea walls built, the last in 1963.

Goldcliff priory became the property of Eton College in 1462, and on one day every year the salmon fisheries had to send enough salmon to supply the needs of the whole college. Whitson also became the property of Eton College because it belonged to Goldcliff priory. The priory ceased to exist in 1467. Hill Farm is believed to have been built with stone from the priory.

Goldcliff church was built in the 13th century, and is dedicated to St Mary Magdalene. It has a left-hand tower and a sundial above the porch inscribed 'CW 1729'. On the approach to the church Goldcliff's public house, The Farmer's Arms can be found. The first vicar of Goldcliff was Roger de Holbrook in 1349. The records are available from 1724.

In 1606 disaster struck Goldcliff – the Great Flood. It reached between two and three feet high in places. It was estimated that in total over the area there were 'twentie hundred' deaths. In Goldcliff church there is a brass plaque showing the height the flood reached on the walls.

There are approximately 30 farms in the area, the other inhabitants being business people. The land is very rich pasture-land, reclaimed from the sea. Before the war the land was only used to grow hay and to feed the pit-ponies of the valley's mines, but the necessity for farms to become self-sufficient in the Second World War made it necessary for them to keep livestock and grow crops. Today not many grow crops but many still keep livestock.

One of the oldest houses in Goldcliff is The Moorlands, a Victorian house built in 1870 for the Waters family. In the garden, rare trees such as acacia, American oak and Christmas strawberry can be found.

The name Whitson is believed to have originated from White-stone, which was found in many areas nearby.

Whitson church is known only as 'the parish church' as it has no dedication. It was built in the 14th century, with Early English architecture. The tower of the church slants south west, which is believed to be because of the pull of the sea. The entrance has a Norman arch and a consecration cross on its left-hand column. The tower contains two bells, one inscribed 'God save our King and Kingdom and send us Peace W&E 1758' and the other 'Obedite'. The first vicar of Whitson was Dafydd ap Gwyllym in 1535, and the records are available from 1728.

One of the oldest houses in Whitson is Whitson Court, which was built in 1795 for the Phillips family. It was designed by John Nash, who was also responsible for Clarence House, Brighton Pavilion for the Prince of Wales and extensions to Buckingham Palace. the stones used to build Whitson Court were mined from the area.

In 1901 it was used by French refugee nuns and later in 1923 as a school for training young men for missionary work in Africa. More recently it has been a zoological park, which started with ducks for the grandsons of the owner, then the RSPCA asked her to take two baby bears, later leading to a varied collection of different animals. Unfortunately it had to close, the animals being distributed to other zoos, but the tiger remained until its recent death.

There are two legends connected with Whitson Court, one being that there is buried silver and the other that there is a smugglers' tunnel which runs through to Goldcliff.

Until 20 years ago there were two shops and a post office in Whitson. The post office was owned many years ago by a Mr Roberts who had a daughter named Eve. Over 30 years ago the Rev Henry Morgan, rector of Holy Trinity, Newport wrote about the legend of Eveswell and how it got its name.

'When Eve Roberts died at The Farmer's Arms, Goldcliff, the other occupants of the inn became troubled of nights. The clashing of furniture, the rattle of moving dishes on the dresser, the clank of fire-irons on the hearth were followed one night by the sight of a woman in white leaving the inn and walking to the church.

The woman had the features of Eve Roberts. With full ceremony the clergy came with bell, book and candle to lay the phantom. At the moment when her name was called, Eve's ghost appeared and, with the villagers in full cry, fled northwards past Nash church, through meadow after meadow, until she reached Eveswell, where with the villagers hard-pressing her, she flung herself into the waters, sank, and was never seen again. And so the well became Ffynnon Eva –Eve's Well.'

Govilon 🦚

Like many villages in this part of Gwent, Govilon, nestling as it does in the Usk valley, was largely agricultural before the Industrial Revolution in the 18th century and the opening of the canal and later the railway which brought more industry and prosperity to the area. It is believed that the name originates from the Welsh gefailion which roughly translated means force or power, because at one time there was a nail factory in the village and a flour mill in Mill Lane. This old building is now a dwelling house but still contains the workings of the mill and the water wheel has been restored.

One of the oldest buildings is Llanwenarth chapel which was built in 1695–96 and was the first Baptist chapel to be built in Wales. The graveyard backs onto the canal and it was the custom to convey the corpse by barge for burial.

The parish of Llanwenarth was divided into Llanwenarth Ultra and Llanwenarth Citra in 1865 and Govilon is in the parish of Llanwenarth Ultra. The present church, Christ church, stands on the site of a small chapel of ease which dated from 1840. A wooden bridge over the river Usk once connected the two parishes and it is recorded that a certain Dassie Morgan made provision for its repair in the sum of ten shillings in 1620! A ferry eventually replaced the bridge and was in use until the 1950s. When the river is low, part of the wooden skeleton of the old ferry boat is visible above the water.

The Church of England also established a National school in about 1860. This was known as Llanwenarth Ultra primary school and was leased to Monmouthshire County Council but still linked with the church. It was closed in 1969 when the new school was opened nearer the centre of the village. The old premises are used as a field study centre for schools in Kettering.

Govilon was well served with public houses in the 19th century when there were 19 in the village! Today, two remain – The Lion (a Georgian building) and The Bridge, which is situated just below the Brecon to Newport canal. This was extended from Gilwern through Govilon to the wharf at Llanfoist in 1806 and was used as a commercial thoroughfare by horse-drawn barges.

Today it is used for leisure purposes and the Govilon wharf is home to Govilon Boat Club, formed in May 1970, where boats of many shapes and sizes are moored. Originally, Govilon wharf was a dock used for carrying out repairs to canal barges and the old stocks used were removed in 1967.

Bailey's tramroad from Nantyglo ironworks came down the hillside in the Clydach valley to the wharf at Govilon and part of this was absorbed by the Merthyr, Tredegar and Abergavenny Railway in 1859. The line was opened in 1862 for the transport of goods and passengers and this caused a decline in the use of the canal and tramroads. At its peak, the new railway line became a prosperous source of employment to the village and at least one-third of the inhabitants worked for the company. The line was closed in 1958 and part of the track has recently been made into a nature walk.

In the centre of the village stands Carpenters Row, today a row of bungalows but originally the site of a carpenter's shop known by the locals as 'The Wheelwright's'. Horse-drawn carts were made and repaired on the premises. The wooden wheels after assembly were bowled down the hill to the blacksmith's shop and banded with an iron rim.

The village still has a blacksmith, who has been involved in that work for some 24 years, having learnt his trade in Ebbw Vale steelworks. It is a lovely sight to see the horses tethered waiting to be shod.

Govilon has expanded through the years with new houses being built but has kept a 'village feel' with pretty cottages and country lanes and by still having the local village stores, post office/stores and a butcher's shop and, of course, the primary school. There is an agricultural community but, apart from the blacksmith, no industry remains. Residents travel to work either in the valley areas of Ebbw Vale/Brynmawr and Cwmbran/Newport or in Abergavenny, the local market town. There are numerous societies active in the village including Brownie and Guide packs, and the village hall is well used.

Grosmont 🎕

A small pictorial booklet printed at the beginning of the 20th century described the village of Grosmont as 'nestling among the hills and as yet undisturbed by the whistle of the iron horse'. A modern visitor to Grosmont might be tempted to think the description still apt. But, peaceful though it looks – a picturesque cluster of pinkish-grey sandstone and painted houses at the foot

Church of St Nicholas, Grosmont

of the Graig Hill and overlooking the river Monnow – Grosmont conceals an eventful and important past.

The ruins of a 13th century castle built by Hubert de Burgh, Justiciar of England, and the name of Grosmont (in French the word means 'great hill' and may refer to the Graig Hill) indicate that the settlement here was created soon after the Normans arrived in England and began their penetration into Wales. The first castle they built was wooden but it was soon replaced by a stronger building in stone.

Grosmont became an important part of the defence of the Norman kingdom and was part of the Marcher lordship of the Three Castles, along with Skenfrith and White Castle. As more peaceful conditions came to the Welsh Marches, Henry III granted the castle to his second son Edmund, whom he made Earl of Lancaster. His descendants, who later became dukes, used it mainly as a residence from which they hunted deer in the royal oak forest of Grosmont. There is a legend that the House of Lancaster took its emblem of the red rose from roses found growing in Grosmont. If it is true, they may have been brought here originally by Eleanor of Provence, the much-loved queen of Henry III. It is certain that until comparatively recently some local farmers paid one red rose at midsummer instead of rent to the lord of the manor. The castle became a casualty of the Wars of the Roses and was mutilated and deserted at the end of the 15th century.

The fine church of Grosmont, renowned not only for its distinctive spire but also for its disused old nave, mirrors the architectural history of the castle, the earliest part dating from the end of the 12th century but most having been built in the 13th century. Queen Eleanor was commemorated by a chapel which formerly adjoined the chancel. The great size of the church always puzzles visitors but it is a reminder to us that Grosmont was once a larger place than it is today. The medieval town that grew up near the castle required a large church but by the 19th century it was much too big for local needs and its size was reduced. At the same time, the interior was rebuilt to make the tower safe. The old nave, however, has been left just as it was when it was first built.

Although this previously important town eventually declined it gave way to the village that we know today. The burgesses who had been settled in Grosmont by the lord of the manor acquired land in the surrounding countryside, first in open fields but by the 15th and 16th centuries they were able to build themselves farmhouses on their land and their places in the village houses were taken by artisans and craftsmen. While the farmers continued their traditional way of life, raising livestock and cultivating the fields, all the trades you might expect in a rural market town could once be found in Grosmont, not only tilers, masons, tanners, blacksmith, farrier, wheelwright and malster etc, but also weavers, tailor, glover, milliner and many more. Walter Powell of Llantilio Crossenny wrote in his famous diary in 1650 that 'the tailor of Grosmont came to work my best suit and cloak.'

But like the markets and fairs that were so much a part of country life until the early 20th century, all these trades have now disappeared again from Grosmont – last to go was the village blacksmith, although John Bryan and his assistant Harry Jones, still remembered by many, have left two handsome gates in the village as their memorial. Today's residents follow many professions – teachers, architects, planners, nurses, builders, mechanics, caterers, butchers etc – but most have to travel out of Grosmont to their work each day.

Two important buildings in local life dominate the centre of Grosmont – the Town Hall and the Angel Inn. The former reminds resident and visitor alike of Grosmont's proud history while The Angel continues to minister to their present needs. Two other public houses – The Greyhound and The Duke of York – have become private houses. A mile away on Cupid's Hill the undertaker and former builder, Joe Godding, still presides at Cupid's Inn.

From time to time Grosmont provides the setting for a cultural event, usually with an historical theme. In 1962 Gwent Federation produced an historical pageant in which many of the county's Women's Institutes took part. In 1982 a local group organised a medieval feast and the following year took part in the Welsh Festival of Castles with a varied programme of events. More recently Morris dancers have begun to make regular visits and drama students have used the castle for performances of Shakespeare.

Stories and legends abound in Grosmont folklore. The most colourful of these concern a character who lived in the reign of Henry V called Jack of Kent who seems to have waged a continuous war against the Devil and who, when he died, is said to have been buried half in and half out of Grosmont church. No one seems to know who he was for certain, but some say he was a priest, or a Franciscan friar or even that he was the same person as the Welsh poet Sion Kent. Some people will also tell you that the castle is haunted by a grey lady but you are more likely to be captivated by the primroses or the glow-worms if you take a walk there.

Henllys 🦋

Henllys, which is Welsh for 'Old Court', stretches from the Nantymilwr brook in the north of the parish to Bettws in the south. It is a very old village – though one can perhaps hardly call it a village as it has no real centre. It straggles the road through from Rogerstone to Cwmbran, sheltered by the Mynydd Maen range with farms dotted on the hillside. There is St Peter's church in the south and a Baptist chapel in the north and between the two at Castell-y-bŵch, the Zoar chapel, now obsolete; a school, two public houses and a village hall.

As a village it was very close-knit: the church and chapels were well attended, there were weekly dances in the hall and whist drives in the winter, every August a sheep dog trial at Cock-y-North (where the new housing estate Pant-yr-haul Close is now), a Hedging and Ditching Society, ploughing matches, Young Farmers, Young People's Guild, Sewing Guild, and of course the WI. One headmaster started a Mutual Improvement Society in the 1930s. People were very poor because of the unemployment and so one shilling a year was charged; they had lectures and important speakers. At that time too a male voice choir was formed, a Mr Albert Cocker the conductor. They competed in Eisteddfod and won a prize.

During the war an army camp was stationed at Graigllwarch Farm. Life became more exciting. The soldiers attended the 'sixpenny hop' dances at the hall, as well as chapel on a Sunday morning. One night the searchlight at the camp received a direct hit but only four cows were killed and luckily no human being since it was a Saturday night and most of the soldiers were at the dance. The next day people walked up to see the devastation. People at that time worked in the colliery at Cwmcarn, Girlings, in Cwmbran and for the 'War Ag', Saunders Valve, and Weston Biscuit Factory.

Then, on a peaceful Wednesday morning in September 1972 it came over the radio that Cwmbran Development Corporation were to extend Cwmbran into Henllys. The next day a public meeting was called and a fighting fund set up to stop the intrusion, but in 1978, after a public enquiry, we lost the day.

The New Town has brought mixed blessings. The green fields have vanished under massive housing developments. There has been an exodus of people who sold properties to the Cwmbran Development Corporation; Zoar chapel has closed; the road through Castell-y-bŵch is too dangerous to walk with an endless stream of cars; the sheep dog trial grounds are no more; the village school has closed. People are employed, not in farming or mining but in factories and school teaching. There is a doctor, and a dentist in the village. A bus runs through every hour. They've removed the postbox from the school, and placed it on Henllys Way. A new hotel, the Baroness has been built. The housing development has done well for the public houses and the Castell-y-bŵch retains its rural views. There is a playground whereas before the children had the fields to play in.

Kilgwrrwg ✺

Until relatively recently Kilgwrrwg was known by the Welsh spelling of Cilgwrwg. There are two possible derivations of this difficult (to the non-Welsh tongue) but interesting name, both of which seem eminently appropriate. 'Cil' is back or a niche as in a mountainside, 'cwrwg' is a coracle, hence 'coracle back'. Anyone standing in the valley by the ancient church and looking up at the ridge along which are spread the scattered settlements of Kilgwrrwg, will readily visualise this ancient image of an upturned coracle. Equally interesting though, is the translation of 'cil' as a cell, as in a hermit's cell, so the name could mean 'Cwrwg's cell', a possible reference to the first Celtic hermit who settled in this isolated spot.

Much available evidence points to Kilgwrrwg church as being of Celtic origin. The church sits on the valley floor atop a slight rise, alone in a field and accessible only by a footpath from the nearest public road half a mile away. Around it lies a circular churchyard adorned by a carved 11th century cross. All these physical characteristics suggest a Celtic origin, together with documentary evidence of a grant of land in the area to the see of Llandaff in AD 722. The original church would probably have been wooden or wattle and daub, perhaps replaced by stone in medieval times and considerably altered in the 15th or 16th centuries.

Kilgwrrwg has always been a poor church, a reflection of its isolated position and sparse surrounding population. Services were generally infrequent and poorly attended and the church has more than once been allowed to fall into severe disrepair. At the beginning of the 19th century the roof had again ceased to be weatherproof and the church was regularly used as a sheep fold except for those twelve Sundays in the year when there was a service. Shortly after this, however, the church was considerably restored and the frequency of services increased, thanks entirely to the combined efforts of the then assistant curate of Kilgwrrwg, William Jones, and his friend James Davies, the famous schoolmaster of Devauden.

The 20th century population of Kilgwrrwg places high value on its ancient church, and extensive fundraising continues to be necessary to restore and maintain the fabric of this unique little building.

The churchyard became the last resting place of one Able Seaman Richard Morgan, who died on Armistice Day 1918 and who was said to be the last British serviceman to die in the First World War.

Kilgwrrwg remains a scattered village of isolated houses. The oldest house is Great Kilgwrrwg farmhouse, the nearest building to the church and constructed in the early 16th century. The majority of later houses were constructed on the ridge above the church. One of these was a public house from 1846 to 1936, officially called The Kilgwrrwg Arms but known locally (even today) as the 'Ramping Cat'. This is a disparaging reference to the inn's sign, intended by the publican to be a heraldic lion rampant but which to many local people looked decidedly more mundane.

The village is also distinguished by having its own Charity field, the origins of which are sadly lost in time. However, it is still administered by a committee of local residents who are required to use the income 'to assist the poor of the parish'.

Today the population of Kilgwrrwg barely exceeds 60; some still involved in agriculture, forestry and local industry, but many others of whom necessarily work away from the immediate area. However, there is a sense in which for local people the ancient church remains an unchanging focus of life in a constantly changing world.

Langstone 🐚

Early in the 10th century, the village was known as Villa Segan, or 'land of the swamp'. The Lord Marchied ruled from his hall, probably where Langstone Court stands today, which in the dim and distant past was a Roman burial ground. Apart from Villa Segan, he also owned the villages of Catsash and Llanbedr, over which he ruled in comparative peace and prosperity. When Marchied died, his wild and arrogant son, Asser, inherited his father's wealth and ruled well enough as long as his every whim and desire were gratified.

It is said that Asser yearned after the beautiful wife of a lesser Lord Gladgwyn, in the service of the lord of Kemeys. When she rejected his advances he became very angry and decided to carry her away by force, after first planning to kill her husband. This he did by bribing one of Gladgwyn's men to loosen a shoe of his master's horse, then when the horse went lame whilst out hunting, the groom was sent off to fetch another horse. When the two men were left alone, Asser drew his knife on Gladgwyn, killed him, and hid his body under the bushes for the wolves to devour. He then rushed to capture the beautiful lady, only to find she had gone away in fear of him. Asser fled the country, leaving all his lands to the see of Llandaff by way of reparation for his crime. The villages of Segan, Catsash and Llanbedr, combined, made the village of Longstone or as we know it today, Langstone.

Langstone derived its name from the 'longstone', two feet in height by four feet square, the remains of which lie in a field near Langstone Court, just off the main road. Not far away is the village church, which remains unnamed. This has three periods of building, part in the 1300s, extended in 1622, and again in Victorian times. The churches of Llanmartin and Wilcrick are also served by the vicar of Langstone.

The village lies approximately five miles from Newport and spreads along two miles of the main A48 road, with several side roads which join up with the original Roman road running from Llanbedr to Catsash as it started the uphill journey across the ridge to the Roman fortress of Isca, nestling in the Usk valley four miles beyond. This road enjoys some of the most splendid views in the county, across the Severn to the Mendip Hills to the south, and to the north, the Black Mountains.

The children of Langstone and surrounding areas are able to enjoy this scenery, as the junior school is situated in Old Roman Road. A very large golf course is also being built further up this road by one of the large hotels. Running on from this road is Cobblers Pitch, a steep little hill, so named because the cobblers

Langstone church

walking out with their wares between Newport and Cardiff when this was the main road, used to pitch their camp here.

A past resident known to all as 'Hack' was a parish councillor and past chairman of Monmouthshire County Council. He was presented with the MBE by the Queen, and will surely go down in history as 'The Father of the Parish'.

Two trunk roads intersect to the west of the village – the M4 London to West Wales road, built to link with the Severn Bridge in 1966, and the A449 road which runs to the north. Here are three large hotels. The local inn, built as a hostelry early in the 19th century, is now the New Inn Motel and caters for all travellers' needs.

We boast several farms, market gardens, and large garden centres. A Mr Alfred Palmer, who, with his brothers came here in 1919 as market gardeners, instigated the building in 1927 of the Methodist chapel in Catsash road. The village shop/post office was originally known as 'The Cabin'. A small wooden building, this was extended some 20 years ago to the prominent building it is now.

Several housing developments have sprung up in the last few years, thus increasing the number of inhabitants. Most people commute to Newport, Cardiff or further afield to work. The village hall was built in 1949 and is used by local societies and groups. A monthly newsletter is published by the village hall committee, which keeps all residents well informed of local news and events.

Little Mill

Little Mill is situated halfway between Pontypool, in the industrial area of the county, and the market town of Usk. At the beginning of this century Little Mill was a thriving agricultural and industrial hamlet, which got its name because its corn mill was smaller than the neighbouring ones at Nantyderry and Usk.

The well known Little Mill bricks were made at the brickworks lying a little to the west of the residential part of the village. The brickworks was served by the GWR at Little Mill junction on the main line from Newport to Shrewsbury, the junction being a single track line from Little Mill to Monmouth. The railway sidings also provided a coal yard.

The road from Pontypool enters the village under the railway bridge, and amongst the first houses, a small engineering works run by the Wilks family was busy making various products including manhole covers. In the centre of the village by the Berthin brook was a tannery shed, with its accompanying cobbled courtyard with workers' cottages on one side and larger overseers' houses on the other.

The mill used by the local farmers for the grinding of their flour and cattle feed, also used the water from the Berthin, the mill race running from the tan-yard alongside the road and over the mill wheel before returning to the brook.

Opposite the mill, and a field away, stands the grey stone buildings of a reform school. The Reformatory, as it was known, was a place of correction for boys who had committed minor offences and was in use until the 1920s, since when it has been converted to private housing.

The local hostelry, having in earlier times been a staging post for coaches travelling between Pontypool and Usk, is aptly named The Halfway House and no doubt for the convenience of stabling and replacing cast horseshoes, the smithy stands adjacent to it. The forge, smithy and wheelwright's shop were busy with agricultural repairs until late in the 1950s.

Between the wars the village consisted of about 40 houses, and during this period a chapel was built and a shop, a post office and a telephone exchange were opened, but the most notable addition was the construction of the village hall, built by volunteer labour during the depression. This was organised by the village policeman, PC Taylor, who delegated jobs to all who crossed his path. He retained a strong interest in the hall long after his retirement. By this time the tannery had stopped work and the houses had been let to local families. The tannery shed was commandeered for use as an emergency mortuary during the Second World War.

Following the war the village entered a period of growth and prosperity. Council houses were built, primarily for agricultural workers, and this led to further private development, 100 houses being built in the 1970s.

The mill ceased to function and the engineering works closed but the tanning shed found yet another use as a studio for a local artist. A local family moved into property in the centre of the village and established a very successful market garden. At this time the residents were enjoying an hourly bus service between Pontypool and Usk.

In recent years Little Mill has completely changed in character. The rail junction and the brickworks have closed, the blacksmith's shop, the foundry and the market garden have disappeared to be replaced by houses. The mill has been converted to a private house, even the shop and the post office have both closed. The farmer in the village no longer farms in the traditional way but provides excellent accommodation and evening meals. The bus service has been reduced to a very limited service.

The village hall and the recreation ground, the chapel and the pub still cater for the social life of the villagers but Little Mill has become a dormitory. The older, longstanding residents are comfortably housed in bungalows for the elderly but mostly the residents are families who travel to the nearby industrial areas for their work and relaxation.

Llanddewi Rhydderch

This small village lies beside the parish road about one mile south of the B4233 Abergavenny to Monmouth road, approximately four miles from Abergavenny. The name Llanddewi implies a dedication to St David. Rhydderch was the Welsh chieftain who ruled in these parts when the Romans came.

At the end of the war the 'village' consisted of the church, vicarage, the school, Church Farm and four cottages. Four council houses were then built, followed a few years later by four more. Then 25 new houses were erected including a new vicarage.

The church, which is over seven centuries old, has one of the finest of Gwent's timbered towers and the yew tree in the churchyard is reputed to be as old as the church itself. There is also a Baptist chapel on the outskirts of the village and a service is held in both every Sunday.

The old British school became derelict but has now been restored and is a private dwelling named Pwll-y-Carw (Pool of the Deer). A new church school was built in 1867 but was closed in 1991. The primary school children now attend Llantilio Pertholey or Cross Ash schools. The senior children attend King Henry VIII comprehensive school in Abergavenny.

On the Saturday following the final closure of the village school, a reunion of former pupils was held and was attended by a large crowd, including some evacuees from Folkestone who had lived with local families and attended classes in the village hall during the war. The oldest ex-pupil, Mrs Mabel Martin, who lived at Tresaison Farm, presented each child with a keepsake. A collage made by the pupils was presented to the vicar. It has now been framed and hangs in the church.

There is no regular bus service, no shop or post office, so cars are essential for shopping and travelling to work. The village people work in shops, offices and factories in the local towns and in mixed farming. We have our builder and plumber, but a high percentage of the local people are retired.

At one time there were three public houses in the neighbourhood, but these have all closed and the nearest 'local' is now in the adjoining village of Llanvapley. The village hall was rebuilt in 1987 and is used for WI meetings, Sunday school and all types of social events including short-mat bowls and a monthly social evening.

Most of the land is privately owned, but Court Farm, the house of which is now derelict, belongs to the Clytha estate and is let to local farmers.

One of Llanddewi Rhydderch's well known 'sons' was the late Dr Emlyn Lewis, one of the first plastic surgeons at St Lawrence's Hospital, Chepstow. His mother was headmistress at the school for many years and is best remembered as a strict disciplinarian.

Another character well remembered was the pig butcher, Mr Jack Prosser who, for many years, 'lived rough' in barns on local farms and killed pigs for farmers and smallholders, providing many home-cured bacon breakfasts for the farming folk.

One of the old customs was the crowning of the May Queen. The children chose a May Queen and King, with the smaller girls as attendants, and made crowns and garlands with spring flowers. They paraded from the school to the village. This event took place on the first school day in May. Sometimes a maypole was erected and the children danced around it holding coloured ribbons. This custom died out some years ago.

Llanddewi Rhydderch is quite a small village, but 'large' in friendship and community spirit. In times of difficulty everyone can be depended upon to pull together. After all, this is what village life is all about.

Llanddewi Skirrid 🌿

Llanddewi Skirrid means the church of St David by the Skirrid, Ysgyrrid Fawr (Great Skirrid) being the name of the Holy Mountain, ysgyrrid comes from the Welsh word 'ysgyren' – a splinter. Legend tells us that Ysgyrrid Fawr was rent in twain (or splintered) during the hour of darkness after the crucifixion. This may be the reason for the title 'Holy Mountain' but another reason may be that during the religious persecution there was a chapel on the highest point.

Another story about the mountain is of Jack O'Kent and the Devil. The Devil said the Malvern hills were higher than the Sugar Loaf and Jack O'Kent bet him that the Sugar Loaf was higher. When the Devil found out that he was wrong, he was taking an apron full of soil to put on the Malvern hills but as he got level with Ysgyrrid Fawr, the cock crowed and his apron string broke and the soil fell out and formed the bit at the end known as Little Billy.

Court Farm at Llanddewi Skirrid was once a monastery. The church was rebuilt in Victorian times by the ironmaster, Crawshay

Bailey. He owned Llanddewi Court and a number of other farms in the area. He is buried in the churchyard there. An old schoolmaster at the time wrote the following poem:

'Tis said the brightest roses
Fade long before their time
And so it seems men dearest
Die even in manhood's prime

One more such friend has vanished
And he was kind and true
he loved his neighbours better
Than many often do

Besides the road's a fountain
The thirsty horses claim
And drink the cooling waters
Placed there in pity's name

In Rhondda's busy valley
And in Gavenny's town
He reigned in hearts of thousands
A king without a crown

But where the wavelets ripple
Across the Irish bay
And far from all loved faces
He passed from earth away

Within Llanddewi's churchyard
And near his well loved town
With Skirrid watching over
They laid the great man down.

And oft on Sabbath evenings
When tolls the service bell
His spirit may revisit
The church he loved so well.

Crawshay Bailey lived at Maindiff Court and the fountain mentioned is in the wall of the hospital now on the B4521, Skenfrith Road.

The Walnut Tree Inn, the world famous Italian restaurant, run by Franco Taruschio is on the roadside in the parish. Thirty years ago it was a very ordinary village pub but Franco's superb cooking has made it one of the best eating houses in the country.

The village which is opposite The Walnut Tree and runs up the hill is Bryn-y-Gwenin – hill of the honeybees. Once this village had a chapel, shop and post office; now it is just a group of houses.

Llandegvedd, Llanddewi & Coedypaen 🦢

Llandegvedd Reservoir occupies a steep valley called Cwmbwrwch through which flows the upper part of the Sor brook. The completion of the dam in 1964 flooded not only this valley but a smaller one called Ysgybor y Cwm (or colloquially 'Skippy Cwm') and four farms, two of which, the Pettingale and Green Pool have given their names to areas around the lake. The reservoir is named after the village of Llandegvedd some two miles downstream. The lake occupies 434 acres but has only a small local catchment area. The bulk of its water supply is pumped from the river Usk and diverted up to the Sluved treatment works on the west bank. From here the reservoir supplies Cardiff and South Gwent, including the steel works at Llanwern.

The reservoir is managed by Welsh Water Land and Leisure. It is the most important stretch of water in Gwent for wintering wildfowl and is renowned as one of the finest trout fisheries in Wales. Recreational uses include fly fishing, sailing, canoeing, windsurfing and training in sub aqua. There is a popular picnic area, nature trail and a seat dedicated to Gwent writer Fred Hando.

The two small villages of Llandegvedd and Llanddewi lie next to each other near the reservoir. The countryside is agricultural and fairly hilly and is watered by the two streams Sor and Candwr.

Both villages are quiet. Up to about 1960 Llandegvedd was cut off from the main road by a water splash and only pedestrians had the use of a footbridge over the Sor brook. The village has developed as a strip and contains a mixture of old and new housing. Some cottages were built by a Quaker, Peter Scott, to provide housing and employment for out of work miners. He lived at Cwrt Perrott, a 17th century house bearing the date 1683 in plasterwork. This was formerly the home of the Rev Gregory Perrott, who became rector of the parish in 1719. Another prominent building is the Bell House, part of a house called Waun-y-pwll formerly occupied by the Ambrose family.

The church is dedicated to the female saint Tegvedd who is reputed to have been martyred by the Saxons. It was founded in the 12th century and restored in 1875–6 in a true attempt at the original. An enormous human leg bone was discovered in the south wall during restoration. This has been inevitably linked with St Tegvedd and it has been estimated that this would have made her eight feet tall! The church contains a medieval vestments chest and the parish bier. The pub, The Farmers' Arms is situated somewhat out of the village, over the Sor which is the old parish boundary, and is actually in Llanddewi.

Llanddewi is a very scattered settlement. Its church, dedicated to St David, was rebuilt in 1857 and joined to the living of Llandegvedd in 1888. The east window was also removed and resited at Llandegvedd. The church is now in private ownership and has been converted into a dwelling. The old rectory at Llanddewi was formerly the home of Arthur Machen while his father was rector there. Among this famous Gwent writer's many works were several references to his happy childhood village. Other prominent houses were Llanddewi Court, home of the Lewis and Wilmot families, and Llansor, built in the 15th century and home of the Meyrick and James families. This beautiful building has two wings at right angles to each other, one wing having originally been stables and outbuildings.

Coedypaen village is also known as Common Coedypaen, a reference to the commonlands which were enclosed in the early part of the 19th century. It is actually much nearer to the reservoir than Llandegvedd is. The church appears to form the village centre although it was only founded in 1848, having been built on land given by Miss Rachel Morgan of Pantygoitre and endowed with £1,000 by Iltyd Nicholl of The Ham, Glamorganshire. It is served by the rector of Llangybi and is called Christchurch. The pub, The Carpenters' Arms, formerly had a blacksmith's shop attached to it which the publican operated.

A school was founded about 1850 in association with the newly built church. Early head teachers included Benjamin Matthews; Joseph Webber, who transferred to Llangybi school in 1865; Job Smith; Clara Webber, Joseph's daughter who had originally trained as a milliner; and, by 1894, Sarah Jones. The school thrived up to the end of the last century with up to 100 pupils but by 1900 the attendance had dwindled to only 20 children and it eventually closed.

There is the usual mixture of old and new housing in the village. On the outskirts, Cilwrgi Farm has a 16th century farmhouse. It is a working farm owned by the Home Office and is linked to Prescoed Young Offenders' Institution. The farm has a reputation for pig breeding. There was formerly a garden centre and rare breeds farm in the village.

Llandenny 🦌

'Llandenny should be of course "the church of St Denny" but is referred to in the Book of Llandaff as "Mattenni". Unfortunately there was no St Denny or Tenni and so the derivation of the name must remain obscure' – so wrote the late Fred J. Hando.

The village of Llandenny lies three miles from Raglan and four and a half miles from Usk. Should you be travelling on the old road between Raglan and Usk, you will find four or five signposts to Llandenny. But beware! you could find yourself in a maze of lanes and return to the main road never having reached Llandenny. It is better to approach the village from either the Raglan–Chepstow road or the Usk–Chepstow road.

The village has about 30 houses in close proximity to the church and pub. However, the parish of Llandenny is widespread and includes Kingcoed, Llandenny Walks and several farms. When anything happens in Llandenny, it includes the whole parish. Church members and WI members come from all corners, as do helpers for any village events.

The village has no shop or post office but there is a pub. This is The Raglan Arms, taking its name from Lord Raglan whose house, Cefntilla Court is set in parkland on the outskirts of the village. Cefntilla Court was bought in 1858 by fellow officers, admirers and friends of the first Lord Raglan and Commander-in-Chief who died whilst on active service in the Crimean War. In an earlier war, it was in the dining room that the Cromwellian commander, Colonel Fairfax, received the surrender of Raglan Castle after a bitter siege, conducted from this house. The present Lord Raglan is very generous in allowing many local charities to use his home and grounds and he takes a great interest in events in the village.

The parish hall was originally a school built on land given by the Duke of Beaufort in 1858. A cottage was attached for the schoolmaster or schoolmistress in charge. The school closed in the 1950s and became a parish hall in the gift of the Duke of Beaufort who decreed that the hall should be administered by six trustees. These should be made up of the vicar and his two churchwardens and three other people elected from the parish. The hall has had its ups and downs! It has seen many happy gatherings and celebrations – whist drives; table tennis evenings; football teas; harvest suppers; and at one stage it housed a playgroup. Thanks to the enormous work of a small committee and helping hands from all over the parish, renovation, redecoration and refurbishment have taken place and Llandenny has a hall of which to be proud.

At one time Llandenny had a railway station on the line which ran from Pontypool to Monmouth. Children were able to travel by train to school in Monmouth. Farmers' wives took their produce to the weekend market in Pontypool and farmers were able to transport stock and the famous Llandenny hay.

Now there is no public transport through the village, but at almost every house there is a car and in many cases more than one. Over the past 20 years the number of cars in the village has more than doubled. So where in the past, most people found their employment in and around the village, or travelled by train to Pontypool, Usk or Monmouth, they are now able to live in the country and travel by car to work much further afield – Newport, Cardiff, Bristol, for instance. As a consequence Llandenny has become something of a dormitory village for people of varying occupations and interests, adding to the richness of village life.

There is a ghost story of a Grey Lady who used to flit amongst the trees on the way down to Cefntilla Court. There has been no reported sighting of her recently!

Some years ago an entire family was murdered at a cottage about seven miles from Llandenny. 'They' say the murderer was a Spanish seaman and he was the last man to be hanged at Usk gaol. What has that to do with Llandenny? Someone from this village, visiting the scene of the crime, brought back a cutting of periwinkle from the cottage garden. This grows along a wall in the village – a reminder that through all the changes which take place, the same plants spring into life each year.

Llandogo

Llandogo is a very attractive village nestling between wooded hillsides about halfway between Monmouth and Chepstow, a couple of miles north of Tintern Abbey. This stretch of the river Wye is considered to be one of the loveliest river valleys in Britain. William Wordsworth, who visited this area on many occasions, wrote about 'the cottages on the hills' and the 'wreaths of smoke' sent up in silence from among the trees.

Llandogo is ideally situated for exploring on foot the whole of the valley between Monmouth and the Severn. The old forests surrounding this village are a particular joy, the youthful fresh greens of spring and the mature red and gold of autumn producing patterns of tint and shade which no artist can emulate.

Llandogo – nestled between wooded hillsides

It is in listening to the old people of Llandogo that the history of the village unfolds. The late Harold Brown was born here at the turn of the century and there have been Browns here for hundreds of years. He was born 'on the very day that salmon fishing begins'. This was appropriate as he was always a keen fisherman and Brown's Hotel caters for the fishermen each year (sometimes the same people year after year). He attended the village school (now the studio home of artist Pat Yallup). In those days before state education, each child had to pay fourpence a week. There were four pubs in the village then including the Sloop (with its entrance facing the river). Now only The Sloop remains (under the friendly ownership of George and Grace).

Llandogo was a port before Chepstow, and many of the local men were barge builders. In those far off days the village was open to much water traffic and had been so for centuries. The flat-bottomed *Trow* travelled the high seas then, carrying cargoes of bark and hazel hoops as far afield as Italy, and bringing back barrels of sherry. The *Llandogo Trow* is immortalised by the name of a pub in Bristol to this day. How idyllic it must have been then when whole families could travel down to Bristol on the outgoing tide and come back on the incoming one.

The railway station which opened in 1886, created great excitement and replaced some of the ponies and traps. It was very sadly missed when Beeching axed the line in the next century.

Mr Brown remembered the Old Farmhouse owned by 'old man Williams' whose wife 'baked wonderful bread'. Mr Brown, with the aid of a donkey called Turpin and pannier bags, carried 'thousands of loaves of bread' along the narrow, high-walled lanes and woodlands to feed the families in the cottages. It was a job he loved and the price was right – threepence a loaf! The high dry-stone walls are a distinctive feature of this valley. They are magnificent and the men who built them must have been Goliaths.

The memories of our church organist at St Ondoceus are vivid. Miss Davies was the organist here for 68 years! She talks happily about the 'holm' (ie the river bank); flower shows of those long ago days of 1928; happy families with lots of children; the fragrant flowers from cottage gardens; the masses of fresh vegetables and huge bowls of brown eggs in baskets. The children would wander down to play on the large, abandoned, solid-oak *Trow* on the river bank.

Talk of the river brought back memories of elvering in the spring, the magic lanterns reflected in the water, the excitement of a delicacy for feeding their families and friends. Elvering had been a traditional activity in this village for hundreds of years, as a social rather than a commercial sport, but if there were any elvers left over they were sold in the Forest of Dean for threepence per pound.

Today elvers from this part of the Wye between Llandogo and Brockweir have become an international, commercial enterprise. Strange men in cars and refrigerated vans come from as far away as Birmingham, stake their claim on the river bank and wait for the incoming tide at 9 pm. The interest in this delicacy is now such that it generated a report on national TV news! The greed for money has spoilt what was a happy annual village event. April and elvering were once synonymous, but sadly we no longer hear the happy voices of the village people. To quote an elderly resident, 'it is the outsiders who are making the money and leaving their litter on our river bank.'

It was in 1954 that electricity came to Llandogo. This was quickly followed by TV and life was changed. The nightingale had to compete with the box. There were even more drastic changes to come. The opening of the Severn Bridge in the 1960s let in a flow of cars and people.

There are however, still many exciting and interesting walks in the vicinity of Llandogo, and the zig-zag walk from the stream on the Cleddon Road uphill to Cleddon Shoots is quite spectacular. There is time to admire and appreciate the trees, the wild flowers and the views as you walk up via the Glen of Llandogo. The zig-zag area is a site of special scientific interest, grade one, and is in the care of the Gwent Conservation Trust. The small hamlet of Cleddon lies at the top, and it was in Cleddon Hall that Bertrand Russell was born. His parents Lord and Lady Amberley used to drive down the zig-zag path in a pony and trap to visit their friends at the house then known as The Falls (now the Priory Nursing Home).

The village of Llandogo derives its name from the founder of the church of St Ondoceus, who was the third Bishop of Llandaff in the 6th century. The present church was built on the same site. Coming to live here in his retirement, the saint founded a monastery and is alleged to have ended his days as a hermit at Cleddon Falls. St Ondoceus is depicted on the pulpit of the local church in the act of saving a stag from huntsmen and hounds in the nearby forest.

This valley is designated an area of outstanding natural beauty, and it is to be hoped it remains so, and that the lines written by William Wordsworth on *Revisiting the Banks of the Wye* will always be appropriate to Llandogo.

Llanelen 🍃

The village of Llanelen is beautifully situated between the river Usk to the east and the Monmouthshire and Brecon canal to the west. The humpbacked bridge over the river is now impossible for the modern juggernauts to negotiate, for it was built in 1821 by John Upton of Gloucester. It replaced a wooden bridge which had been there from time immemorial – Thomas David of Llanelen left sixpence in his will for repairs to the bridge in the early 15th century. The canal was the lifeline for the coal and steel barges travelling to the docks at Newport. It is still negotiable, and boat trips are a peaceful way to view the country.

The village nestles under the heavily forested slopes of the Blorenge, and this, with the views of the Sugar Loaf and the Skirrid, forms a perfect backdrop as you wander through the village 'Wander' is the correct word, for there is no straight road and the cul-de-sacs curve off from the one winding road.

The name Llanelen comes from St Helen's church (Helen being the mother of Constantine the Great). At the turn of the last century, it was purely an agricultural community which boasted the 'big house', Llanelen House. This was the residence of Sir Thomas Phillips, benefactor of the parish, and the Mayor of Newport, who repelled the Chartist Riots. The only remains of Llanelen House are the large stones in a front garden facing the church. The other old buildings include the blacksmith's shop, (now a craft shop) with its adjoining cottages, the school and the school house, the post office and its cottages, and the old vicarage, once the home of Alexander Cordell of *Rape of the Fair*

Llanelen Post Office

Country fame. There was also a parish reading room – now the village hall.

The earliest record of land deeds was in 1497 in the reign of Henry VII; later the manor of Llanelen was a possession of the priory of Abergavenny, but after the dissolution of the monasteries it was granted to the families of Gunter and Westcott in 1546. In 1756 land was given to the vicars of Llanelen, together with a cottage and garden for use as a 'poor house'. With the building of the council houses in the 1940s and and estate in the 1960s, the population has grown from 224 in 1801 to about 900. While still in a purely agricultural area, the villagers now commute to work in the surrounding towns. Llanelen does not possess an inn, though once it boasted three. Lady Llanover, the wife of Sir Benjamin Hall of 'Big Ben' fame, on whose estate Llanelen was situated, closed two of the taverns and turned the third into a temperance house called Y Seren Gobaith (The Star of Hope). She disliked 'strong drink'!

The two focal points of the village are the church and the school. The beautifully kept 12th century church, which is in constant use, still has some old windows and a moulded archway, outside which is an ancient porch. The bell tower, which is a much later Victorian addition, houses two bells, inscribed with the names of two churchwardens, and dated 1652 and 1662. There still remains a projection on the south side showing where the stairs led to the rood loft, and also an ancient base to the font, rescued from the churchyard.

The earliest recorded incumbent was John ap Adam (1385). During the Civil War Cromwell's men were encamped on the slopes of the Blorenge, and the graves of ten soldiers are in the churchyard. It was during this period that Vicar Richard Watkins was deprived of his living by the Puritans for using the Prayer Book (though he was later reinstated).

Education in Llanelen has a long history, for there was a Welsh charity school in the village, which in 1748 had 24 scholars. The present school (still a church school) was opened on 20th September 1862, with tea and buns being provided by its benefactor, Sir Thomas Phillips. The following day 30 pupils were registered, and were found to be 'very deficient in reading and writing'. The first school order included 20 bibles, 134 slates, five pointers, and two yards of flannel at eightpence per yard! The teacher's stipend was £5 per quarter and the monitress was paid three shillings per week. Payment was by results, for in 1869 there was a deduction of one tenth of the grant for 'defective instruction in writing and arithmetic'. Attendance seemed to depend on the weather, potato picking and the Abergavenny Horse Show. An early punishment book lists the number of strokes of the cane – three for stupidity, two for speaking rudely to a man on the road, one for being cruel to a donkey, and one for climbing on the girls' offices. The school is still in use with a headmistress and one teacher and about 40 pupils.

Llanelen has developed considerably over the last five decades, but the open-plan housing development and well kept gardens have given the village a park-like appearance. Consequently it has won the Best Kept Village in Gwent competition on six occasions, and has been second in the Best Kept Village in Wales competition. Borders of shrubs, raised flower beds and seats are the result of monies put to good use because of these successes.

Llanfair & Gobion 🌿

'Llanfair & Gobion' includes the hamlet of Llanfair Kilgeddin and the village of Gobion. It is situated in the beautiful, fertile Usk valley, famous for salmon and trout fishing.

A tumulus sited in a field of Glanusk Farm proved to be a prehistoric burial ground and was used as a sighting point by our ancestors. Remains of Roman pottery have been found in the garden of Gobion Manor, with evidence that a Norman castle once existed in the grounds. First occupied by the Norman Clifford family, and later the Gunters, the coat of arms of the latter and the date 1600 is above the porch doorway. Kilgeddin was mostly held by the lords of Abergavenny as 'demesne lands', transferred on the death of tenants. The name Gobion, from Roman Gobannium, was that of blacksmiths centuries ago.

In 1774 the lord of Gobion manor was granted 'sole royalty of hunting and taking all manner of game within his estate'. In the 1960s Colonel Harry Llewellyn occupied the manor. With his magnificent horse, *Foxhunter*, he brought fame to the village and a 'Gold' for Britain in the 1952 Olympics in Helsinki.

The Crawshay family of Llanfair Court are connected with the iron-masters of Merthyr Tydfil, once world famous as the Welsh metropolis of iron and steel. Captain Crawshay became well known for organising a rugby team of Welsh International players, and was High Sheriff of Monmouthshire in 1939. The Captain's nephew, Sir William Crawshay, now occupies Llanfair Court. He brought honour to the village through his bravery in working with the French Resistance during the Second World War.

Another mansion in Llanfair & Gobion is a Georgian manor called Pant-y-Goytre House. A Dutch baron, Van Moyland, married a Miss Derrington, whose family owned the manor and at one time most of the area.

Two small, ancient churches now serve Llanfair & Gobion. In Llanfair, tucked away down a leafy lane, is the little church of St Mary the Virgin, built on the site of a hermit's cell. The font is 16th century, dated 1577. However, the first parish register is dated 1733. The inner walls are famous for having been decorated in sgraffito, an ancient Italian process, executed by the English artist, Haywood Sumner, in the 1880s, commissioned by the rector in memory of his wife, Mrs Lindsay. The other small church is St Michael's of Llanvihangel-Gobion; the tower being reputedly Norman. The single bell in the western tower is dated 1626. Both churches are in meadows near the river Usk and have suffered from flooding.

Glebe House, in Church Lane near St Mary's church, now a private residence, was originally the rectory for Llanfair Kilgeddin. The rector, Mr Lindsay, also Dean of Raglan, gave the village church hall to both parishes. This hall serves a widespread community in many ways. Church events, school concerts, village fetes, WI meetings, YFC socials, VE celebrations, a pantomime, drama performances, keep fit classes, and recently a bowls club, have all contributed to raising funds to keep the hall in use.

In the same lane is a more recent house called Glebe Barn built by Captain Oram, a survivor of the submarine *Thetis*, which sank in 1939.

St Mary's Hill, on the road to Llanfair Cross, was once the home of Sir Mather-Jackson, the Lord Lieutenant of Monmouthshire. His wife, a Lady in her own right, was a direct descendant of the Duke of Beaufort. Lady Jackson founded the WI movement in Monmouthshire.

Llanfair still has a church school. It is a quaint red-brick building with a school house, built in 1872. One log book records that a Mr Swinnerton and his sister were among a staff of three in 1896, with 80 pupils on the register. Mr Swinnerton became headmaster of the school. His wife lived to be 100 years old. His daughter, Dorothy, is mentioned in Emlyn Williams' autobiography. This kind lady taught him in Holywell county grammar school (Flintshire). When Emlyn Williams left the school she gave him three pound notes. He had won a scholarship to Oxford and she was invited to the university to see him perform in the play *Peer Gynt*.

Schooldays are recalled by local residents. A 'travelling player' with a hurdy gurdy used to entertain them, with a monkey and many tunes. Opposite the school in the front room of the Corner House, Mr and Mrs Chambers (Mum and Dad to everyone), kept the village shop and post office, with a letter-box in the side wall. The children saved their old copybooks for Mrs Chambers. She used them to wrap up her home-made toffee to sell. Each child was given one free piece for their help. Mr Chambers owned a donkey with which he used to go around selling paraffin and other wares. On Good Friday, from 6.30 am, 'hot cross buns' were the special attraction.

An old mill stands beside the forge on the river Pant-y-Belliau, Mr and Mrs Trumper's farm. Pont-Kemys Farm, owned by Mr Brian Jones, dates back to the 16th century. It is situated almost on the banks of the river Usk by the chainbridge , and has survived flooding.

Near the junction with the Abergavenny–Raglan road stood The Herbert Arms. It was a 'spit and sawdust' style house that served the local farming community, and was managed by a Mr Pugh, who had a reputation for bone-setting. This pub is now The Chart House with a restaurant.

The village boasts a very attractive group of agricultural houses built in 1952. About 20 years ago more houses were constructed. The growing population and the increase in car ownership has reduced the once efficient bus service to one bus operating on market day only from Usk to Abergavenny. However, as a result of the growing population Llanfair & Gobion has kept its identity. It has proved to be a delightful place in which to dwell.

Llanfihangel Crucorney & Pandy

The name Llanfihangel Crucorney means church of St Michael, built on a mound. Crucorney was derived from Cruigcornel. Pandy means a fulling mill.

The village stands at the start of the Llanthony valley, through which one passes on the way to Llanthony Abbey and the monastery at Capel-y-ffyn. Each year at the end of August a pilgrimage is made, starting from the church of St David at Llanthony to the shrine of Father Ignatius at Capel-y-ffyn. People from far and wide come to join in this pilgrimage.

In the Middle Ages men kept sheep on the hillside (some still do today). The wool was woven into cloth in the mills. As they do today, they also grew wheat which they would grind into flour at the local mills.

The cattle that they kept were mainly Welsh Blacks which were taken to the market at Abergavenny. Some would also walk the drover's road to Barnet Fair together with farmers and their cattle from mid Wales.

Up until the 1850s the main occupation was farming. Then men got work helping to build the railway line from Abergavenny to Hereford. More schoolchildren went to school in Abergavenny. Prior to the railways they would have to walk, though on market days they would have a lift with people going to market by pony and trap.

The first school in the village was the dame school at The Turrett set up by the Hon Mrs Rodney in 1873; girls from the age of seven to ten years would attend.

The Skirrid mountain was noted for its herds of goats which had very silky hair. In Stuart times this was made into wigs at Abergavenny, then the centre for wigmaking.

The vicar of the parish also kept two or three cows on glebe land. The church had its own tithe barn where farmers would pay their tithes in corn. Meat was salted down in the autumn with salt bought at the Abergavenny September Fair.

In the 19th century Llanfihangel Court was a large estate under the Hon Lord Rodney. Many indoor servants and outdoor workers were employed. Lord Rodney had cottages built for his workmen and he owned much of the land in the village. As they do today, they had their own little garden and grew vegetables. Some would have a row or two of potatoes in a farmer's field.

The first church of St Michael was built on top of the Skirrid mountain or Holy Mountain, as it was called. The present church is 12th century. During the 1970s the roof became unsafe and had to be restored to its present form. There are several interesting memorials in the church. In the porch on the right-hand side is the grave of a blacksmith with the following unusual inscription:

My sledge and hammer lies reclined,
My bellows have lost his wind,
My fires extinct, my forge decayed,
And in ye dust, my vice is laid.
My coals is spent, my iron is gone,
My nails are drove, my work is done.

The east window is by Kempe. Among the panels are the figures of St John the Divine and Queen Elizabeth of Hungary. The features of the Queen of Hungary are those of Imogen Hall whose memorial tablet hangs in the nave, while those of St John the Divine are said to be after Rev Blundell, vicar of this parish for many years.

The church school which followed the dame school was built in 1876. This, again, was replaced by the present school in the late 1970s, but it is no longer a church school.

The village had its own builder, carpenter, blacksmith, painter and decorator, tailor, dressmaker and village shop. There were two fulling mills in the village but no visible signs are left.

The Skirrid Mountain Inn is 11th century and the oldest inn in Wales. Trewyn Manor is another old house in the area and once belonged to the Churchill family.

The local eisteddfod was started many years ago in the school-room before the parish hall was built. People of all ages would come from miles around to compete, from children as young as five years old. The main event was the chief choral competition. This sadly has ceased, but going strong is the annual choral festival which is held in May; interested parties combine to enjoy an evening of popular hymns and solos.

In past years the local flower show was run by the Village Produce Association and the local WI. This is still running, although on a smaller scale and in conjunction with Canau Fete in August.

The population of the village has grown with the building of a new estate. They still have to travel to their place of employment, to Cwmbran, Ebbw Vale, Tredegar and Abergavenny. It is a scattered village. One of the farms (Cefn Farm) had land adjoining the Cefn Court Estate and the field is known as King Charles Meadow.

During the modernisation of the telephone system, the Crucorney exchange became the first automatic exchange in the area.

Llanfoist 🪻

The derivation of the name Llanfoist is obscure, but may originate from the church of St Faith, or from the Latin 'Faustus' meaning prosperous, or perhaps from Fausta who was a 6th century saint.

Rising steeply above the village is the Blorenge (1,800 feet), its lower slopes thickly wooded. Through these woods once ran a tramroad bringing coal and iron to the canal wharf. Limestone was also brought from Blaenafon to the kilns which were situated behind the Llanfoist Inn in the area now known as Kiln Lane.

A spring which rises in the wood above the canal was once a source of water for a brewery situated opposite the church. The brewery has now been demolished but the retaining wall still remains and forms a boundary to the Mountain View housing estate.

At the western edge of the village is Llanfoist House where Crawshay Bailey once lived. He died in January 1872 and is buried in Llanfoist churchyard. A red granite obelisk marks his grave and his epitaph reads, 'A good man obtaineth favour of the Lord'.

The present day inhabitants of Llanfoist are drawn from all parts of the country and many more houses have been built. There is a thriving garage and car sales and a woodyard but the main source of employment is a factory making car components.

Unlike many villages Llanfoist still retains its post office combined with a small shop. Leisure activities are served by a pensioners' association, the Women's Institute, a youth club and a football team.

Two local residents are rapidly becoming well known all over the world; they are the husband and wife team of Charles and Patricia Lester. They design and hand-print luxurious clothes worn by, amongst others, Princess Michael of Kent and Barbra Streisand.

Llangwm 🐚

About four miles south east of Usk on the B4235 road to Chepstow lies the small village of Llangwm. The traveller from Usk may notice the toll house first, and then the Bridge Inn with some cottages opposite. Climbing out of the village, you can see the mill house and, looking back, the former school with windows like a church. But much of what makes Llangwm distinctive lies hidden away from this 'new' road.

The B4235 is the toll road built in 1830. The old road, which had served the village for over a thousand years and probably dated from Roman times, lies about a quarter of a mile away to the east under lane and field near the parish churches of St John (Lower Llangwm) and St Jerome (Upper Llangwm). St John's is an unpretentious Victorian rebuilding of the medieval church of similar size. St Jerome's is the 13th century rebuilding of a church known to have existed in the 8th century, with a crenellated tower added in the 16th century. This large church is now even plainer than St John's as the monuments were removed in the 19th century, but the austerity merely highlights the magnificence of the intricately carved 500 year old rood screen which dominates the nave and draws visitors from far and near.

On the other side of the valley, also at the end of a small lane, stands a simple white Baptist chapel built in 1840 on land given by a descendant of Walter Cradock (1606–1659) who was born in the parish. He influenced south east Wales towards nonconformity during the Civil War, but he is nevertheless buried in St Jerome's church.

Llangwm is Welsh for a community round a church (llan) in a

Llangwm - the churches in the valley.

valley (cwm or -gwm). The other buildings in the village also tell
something of the community, past and present.

Near the Bridge Inn is the church hall, built in 1931 on the site
of the blacksmith's forge. The blacksmith used to be called to the
school next door to try to prevent the stove filling the schoolroom
with smoke, as happened regularly in winter. A former pupil can
remember taking farmhorses to be shod at the forge on the way
to school and collecting them at lunchtime to go home.

The school started as the Llangwm National and Church of
England school in 1871. At its largest in the early part of this
century it taught over 80 children, and a new classroom was
built for the infants who had been managing in a tent during
the hot summer of 1901. The school was closed in 1984, and the

sound of children's voices at play rising from the valley is heard no more. About one and a half miles along the minor road beside the school is the Model Farm erected by the Duke of Beaufort in the 18th century using an innovative cruciform design intended to be a pattern or model for other farms.

Back in Llangwm, the shop and post office have occupied various premises at different times but most recently Brook House, opposite the school and marked by the postbox at the gate. When the postmistress who at one time carried letters round the farms on foot died, a significant part of village life died too.

In Chapel Road going away from the Bridge Inn stands a house built on the site of the forge when it moved from near the school. The name of the house, Tir Efail, means 'smithy-land'. Further along at Llan-y-Nant, stood the carpenter's workshop. He was also the wheelwright, and used to bowl the wooden cartwheels along to the smith who fitted the iron rims. Near Llan-y-Nant a spring emerged which provided the village with drinking water until as recently as 30 years ago. A couple of miles outside the village, along this road, is the Gwent grass ski centre.

Although there are a number of new rural attractions such as the grass ski centre, the predominant land use remains sheep and dairy farming. Farmhouses in the parish are scattered over a wide area and Llangwm is fortunate in having a newly refurbished, easily accessible church hall for the many different social and educational activities which are arranged throughout the year.

Llangybi 🐟

Llangybi, or Llangibby, is a small village in the middle of Gwent between Usk and Caerleon. It lies above the flood plain of the river Usk overlooking Wentwood while, behind, gentle hills rise towards Llandegfedd reservoir. The land is agricultural with some woodland and supports a rich wildlife.

The village takes its name from the Cornish saint Cybi, believed to have founded a church here in the 6th century. A standing stone near the river also bears his name. The present church dates

The White Hart Inn at Llangybi

from the 11th century and contains medieval wall paintings of St Christopher, the Creed and a remarkable Christ of the Trades. There is an unusual double approach to the long-gone rood screen and 17th century font, pulpit and communion table.

In the churchyard is the communal grave of William Watkins of Cefn Llech cottage, his wife and three young children, all gruesomely murdered one July evening in 1878. Joseph Garcia, a 21 year old Spanish sailor, was convicted of the crime and hanged at Usk gaol before an enthusiastic crowd. The Llangybi murders were celebrated in verse and attracted crowds of sightseers from miles around.

Llangybi's old name was Tregrug (the place on the mount) after its castle which dates from the early 14th century. It occupies a wooded plateau above the village, encircling the entire site with a single fortified enclosing wall, probably the largest castle enclosure

in the country. There is also a massive gatehouse and the remains
of several towers but the whole structure is in ruins and covered
in vegetation. Although the castle was garrisoned with 60 men
during the Civil War it was probably never completed and is now
owned by the local estate.

Below stood a handsome 45 roomed 17th century mansion,
possibly designed by Inigo Jones. This was the home of the
local landowner. The Addams Williams family, over generations,
participated in county and national affairs and, as squires of
Llangybi, influenced almost every facet of village life. After 1861
the family let the house and among the tenants was Dr Frederick
Rutherford Harris, former private secretary to Cecil Rhodes, who
set up the coach service between Newport and Raglan. Later the
house became delapidated after use by the armed services during
the Second World War. Restoration and maintenance proved too

expensive and in 1950 the mansion was demolished. Still surviving in its grounds are the remains of Llangybi's oldest castle, a small ringwork fortification from the Norman period.

The most striking building in the village is The White Hart, a former coaching inn once owned by the Knights of St John of Jerusalem. It was used as a campaign headquarters in the Civil War when Sir Trevor Williams served first the Roundhead then the Royalist cause, and prisoners were held in its cellars.

The White Hart and the church together with the busy blacksmith's shop, post office store and a cluster of old cottages form the picturesque centre around the village green. While this scene remains largely unchanged, along the two side roads development has been taking place since the late 1960s.

First came two estates of family-sized homes which led to an influx of children, boosting enrolment at the village school and bringing the setting up of a playgroup, Brownie pack and youth club. This was balanced by the addition of several pensioners' bungalows (with a resident warden) and also a few council houses. Recently there has been infilling and the completion of two small developments of 'executive' housing. The population is now over 400.

Whereas formerly villagers found work locally on the land, now most residents are employed in businesses and the professions and the village has become a dormitory area for neighbouring towns such as Newport, Cwmbran and Cardiff. Even so, farming and related trades are still an important part of the economy. Most of the farms belong to the Llangybi Castle Estate, owned by the Addams Williams family, and are small with a dairy herd of Friesian cows as the main enterprise. Some of the larger farms also have beef cattle and sheep and grow corn.

A few villagers are employed by the Llangybi Hunt, one of the oldest packs of foxhounds in the country. The hunt kennels are situated in the village and there are 30 couples of hounds. The meet on Boxing Day morning at The White Hart attracts large crowds. The estate lets out its shooting rights to a sporting syndicate and pheasants are bred in Tregrug Castle enclosure. The blacksmith's shop is a family business employing five people who undertake farriery, general repairs and ornamental work.

While some aspects of traditional village life continue others have declined. The Baptist chapel has recently been converted into a private dwelling and the village school which opened in 1842 was closed in 1985, to the dismay of all. The children are now taken by bus to schools in Usk and Caerleon. The village hall has been bought recently from the estate after a major fundraising effort by villagers and is being refurbished but there are now fewer organisations using it and even the Women's Institute has a declining membership.

However, the village is fortunate in having an enthusiastic resident rector, a flourishing shop, an active community council, a garage and a bus service. Llangybi enters, and sometimes wins, the Best Kept Village in Gwent contest. Regular events include the bonfire night with fireworks, fun run, footpath walks, jumble sales and the celebrations of Easter, Harvest and Christmas. The pensioners enjoy regular outings by coach and the children have space to play. It is a very pleasant place in which to live.

Llanhennock

Set on the summit of a high ridge on the old Roman road from Caerleon to Usk, in the manor of Edlogan in the Hundred of Usk, the village of Llanhennock, hardly more than a hamlet, is sparsely inhabited, with a cluster of houses and restored cottages around a little square. One of these, 'the house with the wooden leg', was formerly an inn and, it is said, was a resting place for travellers who had crossed the Severn from Bristol in the old ferry boat, the *Llandogo Trow*. This little square crowns the hill and contains, in addition, a village hall, a church which still retains its embattled tower and the old Wheatsheaf Inn, aptly named because it overlooks rolling green pastures and cornfields which lead down to the meandering river Usk, haunt of salmon and trout fishermen and small pleasure craft. The old forge has been transformed into a dwelling house, as has the old school which still, however, proudly boasts the old bell tower.

The landowners were the Mackworths, whose splendid house, the Oaklands, still stands in the village. It has been restored to its former glory after many vicissitudes, having been acquired for an unmarried mothers' home and a home for difficult and deprived children. The old rectory is now a Cheshire Home and is very much part of village life.

It was Sir Digby Mackworth who built Glen Usk, a fine Georgian house, 'its situation Romantic, the gardens and pleasure grounds of great beauty'. Every year in early summer its grounds are thrown open to the public to enjoy its magnificent banks of rhododendrons, its gardens and its peacocks. At Christmas time, thanks to the generosity of the owners, the Burges, a grand Christmas party is held in its lovely hall with glowing log fire, tall glittering Christmas tree and convivial atmosphere, where friends and neighbours are plied with delicious eats and drinks. At about 9pm, the carol singers appear at the door to sing and are soon bidden inside where everyone joins in, and the singers are fed with mince pies and warm punch. It is all very reminiscent of the festivities in Hardy's *Under the Greenwood Tree*!

When Sir Digby Mackworth built Glen Usk in 1820 there was no coach road to it, so he built the present road which runs from the junction of the village for about three miles to the house. The original lodge still stands at the beginning. Several films have been made at Glen Usk using its beautiful location, and even the village itself was once used as a film set and was transformed for the time into an old Welsh village.

The parish boundaries are far-reaching and many old Elizabethan houses lie within its bounds. One of these houses has a secret and ancient priests' hole in which priests hid during the Reformation, for the area was stoutly Royalist and Catholic. Pencraig, now a farmhouse, was built in the early 16th century and was inhabited by an old Welsh family, the Morgans, who left '£5 for the casting of a great bell' in the church. It was in 1686 that the Morgans' granddaughter Mary married Sir Humphrey Mackworth, whose descendant built Glen Usk. Opposite the house stands the huge, historic Caerydor Oak, which has a height of 70 feet and girth of 38½ feet. On high days and holidays, the tree was decorated with yellow ribbons, and the villagers danced and sang around it.

Nowadays the celebrations of national events take place in a field behind The Wheatsheaf. There are races in the afternoon for the children with a slap-up tea to follow in the village hall. In the evening the whole village is en fête, and there is a grand barbecue in the field. Delicious steaks, sausages and beefburgers are cooked by three stalwart men in their chef's garb, the beer tent is well patronised and the villagers sit on trusses of hay and chat and watch Robin Dean's hot air balloon drift lazily across the summer sky. The moon rises, the crowds disperse, everything is cleared away and the world is left to darkness. The next day the village returns to its normal quiet way of life.

There is much that could be said about this lovely old village with its many historic houses: Cwm-y-Wiwer 'the cuckoo's nest' home of the Talbot Laybourne family; Cefn Henllan, with its matey three-seater loo; Soar Mill House, home of the miller of long ago. Originally three cottages, the latter is now a modern house, inhabited by an intrepid Dutch lady and her husband. Intrepid, because during the Second World War she carried anti-German propaganda around Amsterdam in her midwife's bag, under the very eye of the Hun, narrowly escaping detection on one occasion. Tithes were still paid to the owners of Soar Mill House up to 1948.

There are many other houses of interest in the village. Fortunately, local planning officers jealously guard this remaining piece of rural Gwent and long may this continue despite the inexorable march of progress.

Llanishen 🌿

Llanishen is situated high to the left of the ridge between Monmouth and Chepstow with magnificent views over the Vale of Usk to the Mynydd Maen and Blorenge ridge. Several footpaths and lanes enable the walker to enjoy this scenery. Buzzards soar in the sky and sometimes the white-winged gliders from the club near Llandenny below rise in the thermals.

Llanishen was situated at the boundary of one of Tintern Abbey's granges. Farming is still the predominant feature of the landscape. A comparison between the tithe map of 1840 and the present day Ordnance Survey map shows few changes in the roads or variations to the field system. In days gone by orchards abounded whereas today the farming is mainly pastoral. Older inhabitants can recall visiting the well in Vicarage Lane while it was still in use, to 'dress' it with a wreath of box tree leaves on New Year's Day as a thanksgiving for it never running dry.

Llanishen derives its name from the church of St Isan or Nissien, who were one and the same. It is known that there was a wooden church here in the 10th century. Today the patron saint is St Dennis. St Dennis's church was built in 1854. It is the third place of worship on the site, nothing remaining of the previous thatched church. However, the base of the old praying cross still exists and can be found at the lower end of the churchyard. In 1954 the church was redecorated and electricity was installed for the centenary celebrations.

A plaque on the north side of the nave commemorates William Jones of Tregeiriog House, who 'left by his last will dated the 16th day of April 1651, an estate consisting of three fields, lying in the parish of Llanishen containing 18 acres two roods called the poor's land; which estate is to be let according to the law and the money to be given half-yearly for ever, one pound to the parish of Penyclawth and the remainder to the old and infirm parishioners of Llanishen (who are not paupers) at the disposal of the minister, the churchwardens, the overseer and the magistrate acting for the division.' (Pen-y-clawdd is an adjoining parish.) These days the trustees are the vicar and the churchwardens and the beneficiaries are local people with a 'need'.

There is a story that in 1870 the then vicar, James Oakley, took the 1620 Welsh bible from the church and buried it in his garden as he did not know what else to do with it, Welsh no longer being the language used in the church. It was the teaching of Welsh in order to read the scriptures that brought the first schools into

Llanishen. Unhappily the village school was forced to close in 1987. The children now have to travel by bus to the neighbouring village of Trellech where a new school was built to replace five village schools which were closed. Trellech is also where the local health centre is situated.

The village once abounded with a multitude of chapels which have now been converted into private residences. Bethel chapel was the last to close; this lies high up on Far Hill, and held special services until quite recently.

The journey into Trellech takes you past a field known locally as the Bloody Fields, so named after a battle fought between the Cavaliers and the Roundheads. The horses were said to be up to their fetlocks in blood, which flowed out onto the road!

There is an avenue of oak trees along the road to Trellech Grange which were planted to celebrate Queen Victoria's Golden Jubilee.

Llanishen now has only one public house, The Carpenter's Arms, which was built in 1700, a bog on this site having been drained. The front part was added about 1800. They used to bake and sell bread; the old bread oven remains to the right of one of the large fireplaces but much of the public area has been altered in recent years.

Llanishen House was also a public house until the 1960s. In the grounds are the remains of the last working mill in the village. There is still a right of way marked on the map which is the route of an old coffin road leading to the church next door; this now runs through an extension built onto the house!

Llanvair Farm, about a mile from the village, is thought to have been built on the site of a church, as its name seems to suggest, but there is no record of this. The original building dates from the 16th century and has a porch, passage and stairway built out from the house with two landings; the attic was used as servants' quarters. A church door has been used in its construction; there is a gravestone at the bottom of the garden but this is of a more recent owner. When Hubert Harris and his wife Emily bought Llanvair he built the Dukes Farmhouse opposite and today the Llanvair land and Dukes land are farmed as one by his descendants.

Further along the road is Tregeiriog, mentioned earlier; this was the principal residence in the 16th and 17th centuries but references to it first began as early as 1295. Old maps show it as a place name.

The green corrugated iron parish hall was built on the site of an old quarry as a First World War memorial for the three parishes of Llanishen, Llanvihangel-tor-y-mynydd and Trellech Grange. When the school closed the original school clock was presented to the village hall; it was here that the children once came in crocodile file to have their school dinners. An unprepossessing building it may be but it acts as a centre for many activities such as whist drives, dances, Sunday school and a very successful pantomime group, for this scattered village.

Llanover 🌿

The greeting, translated from the Welsh, over the Tudor gateway to one of the lodges guarding the entrance to Ty Uchaf (Upper House), Llanover, reads –

'Who art thou, visitor?
If friend, welcome of the heart to thee,
If stranger, hospitality shall meet thee,
If enemy, courtesy shall imprison thee.'

This was the home of Sir Benjamin Hall who was the first Commissioner of Works and who gave his name 'Big Ben' to the bell at Westminster. A big man in effort and stature, it was he who had trees and flower beds laid out in Hyde Park and it is believed had the railings around the park cast of local iron in nearby Pontypool.

This little gem of a village is set against a background of mountains, amongst the noblest of trees, threaded by one of the finest reaches of the river Usk, and skirted by the beautiful canal running from Newport to Brecon marking the boundary of the Brecon Beacons National Park.

Few can claim that part of their village was built as a memorial. Such was the case here, for the great-grandson of Sir Benjamin Hall (who was created Baron Llanover in 1859) and his talented wife Lady Llanover, was Captain Elidyr J.B. Herbert, who was killed on active service in Palestine during the First World War and his memory was perpetuated, and indeed, that of each soldier of Llanover who gave his life, in houses built around a village green. Through the green an avenue of lime trees leads to an alcove surrounded by 18 pollarded trees, one placed in memory of each of these men and with their name inscribed on a plaque. The whole area is named Tre Elidyr (Elidyr's town).

It is here that the school, built at the same time, continues to further the traditions started by Lady Llanover who, although of English birth, fought for the Welsh traditions in this border county between England and Wales. She had Welsh flannel manufactured in the village, kept a staff of Welsh-speaking servants and fostered the tradition of the triple-stringed harp by employing the services of a blind harpist, Gruffydd Richards. He has been succeeded through the years by many well known musicians, right up to the present with the celebrated Ann Griffiths, who has been known to play Llanover's triple harp at concerts in the nearby town of Abergavenny. This harp is still in the possession of the present owner of Llanover Estate, Mr Robin Herbert. It is at the village school that the Dawns Werin Llanofer (Welsh Reel) is kept alive, danced by the local children in some of the original Welsh costumes made from flannel manufactured at the local woollen mill.

For over 100 years the estate has kept a flock of black sheep, which still graze in front of Ty Uchaf, and this flock has won many prizes in shows all over the country. From these flocks, some folk say, originated the nursery rhyme, 'Baa, baa black sheep'.

Today about 300 live out their lives in this wonderful little haven of by-gone days, bringing the freshness of modern time to the village with an enthusiasm for the village hall activities. The hall now has a bar although until about 20 years ago the village was dry owing to Lady Llanover's aversion to alcohol and her closing of the seven public houses in the village. In the hall are held dances, bingo sessions, badminton, an art group and weekend get-togethers, while the strains of 'Mae Hen Wlad Fy Nhadau' (Land of my Fathers) can often be heard late on a Saturday night.

And so it goes on, history interwoven with today to make a pattern for tomorrow and how better to finish than to repeat the words facing the departing guest as he leaves the lodge gates:

'Departing guest, leave a blessing
On thy footsteps and mayest thou be blessed:
Health and prosperity be with thee on thy journey
And happiness on thy return.'

Llansoy

The small village of Llansoy occupies an elevated position about five miles to the east of Usk. Perhaps the most spectacular way to approach it is to turn off the A466 Chepstow-Monmouth road between Devauden and Llanishen. This road, the Star Pitch, has magnificent views across to the Brecon Beacons. In 1832 this particular route was described as 'long and precipitious', one that made coach travel so tedious that a new, lower road between Chepstow and Usk was built three years later, further isolating the village.

Indeed, Llansoy was quite remote at this time – an agricultural community with most of the farms and cottages barely visible from the road. But despite a population of only about 130 by the 1870s the villagers managed to support a church, a chapel and three pubs, though not necessarily in that order. The chapel has since been converted into a house. The village shop has also closed, the single petrol pump is only a memory, but there is still a post office, now in its third home at The Cwm.

However, in the 1970s the village was given a central focus when a small group of houses were built in a field near the church. The only other major change has been the planting of a vineyard

Church of St Tysoi, Llansoy

and the setting up of a deer farm, both at Cwrt-y-Brychan, one of the oldest farms in the village.

The most ancient feature of Llansoy is the remains of an Iron Age fort at Great House, which is set above the Cross Hands Pitch at the northern end of the village.

The church of St Tysoi dates from the 15th century, although there has probably been a church on the site since the latter part of the 6th century. It has an unusual modern stained glass window which depicts the changing seasons of an agricultural community.

In the churchyard there is a gravestone near the porch, carved with the haunting image of a beautiful young woman above a coiled snake. Ann Morgan, who died when she was only 20, is thought to have been killed by a snake bite in 1835. Another pessimistically morbid headstone near the stile has this epitaph:

'Remember me as you pass by
As you are now so once was I
And as I am so shall you be
Therefore prepare to follow me.'

In 1867 the rector, the Rev Richard Evanson, built a small school – before this lessons were held in the church, possibly in the gloomy belfry. The single school room was used to teach not only 23 local children during the Second World War, but also 21 evacuees from Folkestone. It was closed in 1960 and is now used as a village hall.

School records provide an insight into what life was like for such a close rural community. The school was often closed for a day or the register unmarked because of bad weather. Even quite young children were kept at home during harvest time because an extra pair of hands was needed on the farm. An early memory concerns one of the least respected teachers to have been employed. The villagers were united in their dislike for her and noisily 'drummed' her out of the village, beating pots and pans with great fervour.

The poor of the village were cared for by a charity fund. Money was handed out annually in January and the recipients had to qualify by taking communion three times a year. One popular character of the 18th century, Dorothy Paul, was particularly well cherished by the parish. Records exist detailing regular assistance over 21 years. It began in 1770 when she was voted two bottles of ale and a 'peck of wheat'. In 1773 her house appears to have been thoroughly renovated and rethatched for a total cost of £4 3s and until her death in 1791 she received a succession of gifts of food, cash and material for clothing. The last entry is for a coffin, a shroud and candles.

Although Llansoy has changed from being an isolated, close-knit rural community and there are now many people living there who work elsewhere, it has not lost its essentially rural character. Letters are no longer delivered by foot on a muddy circuit that took Joe the Postman four hours to complete each day, but his route can still be followed and the views are glorious.

Llantilio Crossenny 🌿

Llantilio Crossenny, or as it should more properly be known Llanteilo Croesenny – 'the cross of St Teilo', is set amidst the most beautiful countryside halfway between Abergavenny and Monmouth on the B4233.

The small, rather sprawling village has many historically interesting buildings and evidence of Roman occupation has been found in the area. The present church dates back to the 14th century. The church sits on what is either an ancient burial mound or a natural hillock, its grey shingled spire a landmark for miles around. It is now a symbol of peace and tranquillity but has been the onlooker to many disputes throughout its lifetime, including a past vicar being deprived of his living for 'drunkenness and malignancy' in more puritanical times. He was eventually re-instated, only to die shortly afterwards, and is interred in the chancel of the church. There is a fine peal of eight bells which attracts bellringers from all over the country. Originally there were only six bells and these were recast in 1709; in 1978 they were once again recast after a big fundraising effort by the parishioners and the extra bells were added. The church is noticeable for possessing more than its fair share of burial monuments set into the floor and has what could be known as the rudest parishioner – the Green Man. He is on the western pier of the central arch poking out his tongue to one and all! The Green Man, a figure well known in folklore, was a symbol of new life and resurrection.

Earlier this century the local blacksmith objected to the vicar's idea of moving the headstones to form a boundary wall, making it easier to keep the churchyard mown and tidy. The blacksmith's wife was locally regarded as being a witch and the blacksmith threatened that, 'If the vicar disturbed the family grave, he would disturb the vicar!' It was wisely decided to leave well alone, the vicar fearing that the combined forces of strength and supernatural powers might prove too much for him. The stones sit, to this day, grouped together in the middle of the churchyard lawn. These days the church is famous for the Llantilio Festival of Music and Drama, which is well supported and has many well known artists appearing in it. The festival now lasts for four days and is directed by Mr Charles Farncombe; the programme usually consisting of recitals, light operatic works and choral song, and ending with the Festival Evensong which is always followed by teas provided by the villagers.

The village once had a thriving mill on the river Trothy; this is now a tastefully restored private dwelling. The well known Hostery Inn has been situated on its present site since 1459, but there was an earlier inn nearer to the church – no doubt the reason for the vicar being deprived of his living!

The village has two sites which once held great manor houses, so it could be said to be famous for what it does not have! The Great House, which was sited alongside the church, was demolished earlier this century after having been sold to a steel company in Ebbw Vale by the Mather Jackson family; it was then allowed to fall into disrepair. About a quarter of a mile from the church was the medieval moated site of Hen Gwrt, the home of David Gam, who was lame in one leg and from whose misfortune, they say, came the phrase 'gammy leg'. He had flaming red hair and was said to have fathered so many children that had they joined hands, they could have reached from the church to Hen Gwrt! David Gam (or Daffyd ap Gam) had other claims to fame. He attempted to assassinate Owain Glyndwr in 1402, and he then became famous for his exploits on the battlefield and was knighted by Henry V at Agincourt. Owain Glyndwr eventually burned the manor house, Hen Gwrt, to the ground in reprisal for the attempted assassination. All that remains now is the mast surrounding the acre of ground on which it stood.

The fine 16th century manor house of Cillwch, still in use, has many interesting features. The attic was used as a chapel where mass was celebrated during the persecution, and there is an ancient stained glass window depicting St George and the Dragon. The house also contains much finely carved oak.

The village is overlooked, from a distance of about two miles, by White Castle, one of the Marcher castles which is in quite a good condition. Skenfrith, Grosmont and White Castle were once owned by three brothers, White Castle or Castle Gwyn being lived in by Gwyn. There is some discussion as to whether the name derives from the walls being plastered or painted white or from the name of the person who once owned the castle (Gwyn being Welsh for white). There are fine views of the surrounding countryside from the castle and also a sense of peace and tranquillity. This makes one wonder if this is why it was a favourite 'outing place' for the German, Rudolf Hess, when he was incarcerated in a nearby hospital during the Second World War. The castle is now part of the Three Castles walk with Skenfrith and Grosmont, and the area also has Offa's Dyke footpath running through it, both of which are enjoyed by many visitors.

Llantrissent 🦎

An ancient village growing slightly and changing slowly, Llantrissent has eight times won the Best Kept Village in Gwent competition and once the Best Kept Village in Wales. The greater part of the village is in a loop road, so that most of the traffic avoids this peaceful haven. The houses surround the part-Norman church and large churchyard which contains a large preaching cross. The font is dated 1673, but a priest is recorded back to 1343.

The churchyard is now beautifully kept so that grass snakes, adders, frogs, newts, stoats and feral cats have had to seek new residences. The church would seat about 200 but most Sundays it seats around ten to 15, showing that this is a secular age. The village was once larger but now only a few stones and snowdrops in rows show where people once lived.

The usually quiet stream which runs through the village on its way to the river Usk can, in times of prolonged downpour, quickly change its habit and reach the river via three or four houses. The roads to Usk and Newport flood a few times most years, which stops the buses and gives school-children an extra holiday. Superiority is afforded to drivers of high-based vehicles, to the embarrassment and icy cold feet of those who leave their cars stranded, having misjudged the depth.

Llantrissent has a number of scattered farms, most of which are very old. The village school is now a house. There is a garage and two public houses, but no shop, no mains water, no mains sewerage, very few buses and a certain amount of noise from the nearby A449.

About 150 people live in the village and there are a dozen children, who go to school in Usk, Caerleon or Monmouth. The villagers mostly know each other, are friendly, concerned and helpful. They often combine in joint effort over village occasions.

Llanvetherine 🌿

Llanvetherine is named after a 6th century saint, St Gwytherin. After the Roman occupation when the soldiers all returned to Rome, the Celtic people were left with Christianity and the Celtic Church evolved singularly until 768 AD when it acceded to Rome; but it kept its own characterisation until the Norman Conquest. Many of the saints who have given their names to the churches in our parishes were religious hermits, who firstly built a cell and preached to the Celtic people around them. The cell was enclosed with a wall and this eventually grew into a church and cottages round about. This enclosure became the 'Llan', the church and village.

There is a very large stone slab with the carved figure of St Gwytherin in the church. It was originally in the porch but about 20 years ago the vicar, Rev Michael Hewlett, with the help of the churchwardens and a group of strong men, decided to carry the saint into the church to preserve the stonework. This operation took several evenings and the vicar worked out how many manhours it took to move him. There are also two interesting carved Tudor figures on either side of the altar.

Llanvetherine used to have two pubs, a school, a shop, a post office, a church and two chapels; sadly now only one chapel and the church remain.

Above the village on the hillside stands the medieval fortress of White Castle, a Norman castle built to control the Welsh. It is interesting to read the names of the lords of White Castle in Skenfrith church. It shows how the castle passed from Welsh to Norman lords over the ages.

A lovely story about the castle is of The Blind Knight. Gwyn ap Gwaethfoed was an aged Welsh knight who was lord of White Castle in the reign of William Rufus. Gwyn was blind but this did not prevent him from going hunting and one day when he was away from his castle, a bold Norman baron laid siege to White Castle and took possession of it. When Gwyn returned, he was met by one of his loyal archers who told him what had happened. Gwyn asked the King to allow him to fight fairly for his castle, so a duel was fought in a darkened room in a tower at White Castle. Gwyn slew the English lord and the Normans were sent out of the castle and the blind lord of White Castle proudly took over his castle again.

Rudolf Hess, the German deputy leader in the Second World War, was imprisoned at Maindiff Court. He used to be taken for walks with an armed guard, an officer walking beside him and two armed soldiers behind, over the village of Bryn-y-gwenin and up to White Castle. Hess spent many sunny days sitting on the horn work at White Castle looking at fish in the moat and writing his memoirs. When I was a child I remember him standing by our gate watching us children playing.

Llanvihangel-tor-y-mynydd 🕮

Llanvihangel-tor-y-mynydd, meaning the church of St Michael on the breast of the mountain, lies about 500 feet above sea level. It is on the road from Chepstow to Raglan, six and a half miles north east of Usk and eight miles north west of Chepstow. In 1891 the Duke of Beaufort KG was lord of the manor and principal landowner. The church of St Michael, restored in 1860, is an ancient structure in the Early English style. It consists of a chancel, a nave, a north west porch and a western bell turret containing two bells. The church seats 100 people and the register dates from 1592. In the 19th century there was also a Bible chapel on the summit of the hill.

The oldest house, Church Farm, is the same age as the church, about 800 years old, and is built with oak that was cut on the farm. Llanpill, another farmhouse, built over 400 years ago is at present occupied by the great-great grandson of the Rev John Price who was the rector of the parish from 1846 to 1883 and built the Old Rectory. Joined to Llanvihangel-tor-y-mynydd was the hamlet of Llangunnog with its own church but alas, only a few headstones now remain and the hamlet has been absorbed into Llanvihangel.

The parish contains 1,186 acres – at the turn of the century

St Michael, Llanvihangel-tor-y-Mynydd

there were 35 inhabited houses, six uninhabited and a population of 127. Now, however, there are six derelict houses and the population of 85 occupy 39 houses.

The Star Hill Inn has been in existence since at least the 15th century but the original building has been extended. It is situated on the old coaching route between Chepstow and Raglan where the two coaches, *Nimrod* and *Fusilier*, would stop to change horses. There is a story that an apparition of a coach and horses passes along this road but the present residents have not seen it! At The Star, it was reputed that extra horses were hitched on to the timber waggons to take them up the steep Star Hill.

John Wesley, the Methodist minister, stayed at the Star Inn and described it as 'a good small inn'. The menu nowadays consists of much local produce, including venison from the nearby deer farm at Brecon Court, which also produces wine from its own vineyard.

At the turn of the century there was a small shop at the top of Star Hill where 'Johnny the Tea' sold sweets to the school-children walking to and from the school at Llanishen. Now the shop is derelict and the children are transported to the school in Trellech by bus or car.

There is a footpath that runs from Llanvihangel to Wolves-newton by Llanpill farmhouse. When the owner built an extension which covered the path, the court ruled that any person using the path could demand to walk through the extension, very inconvenient if the owner was not at home! Fortunately, the path has now been diverted around the outside of the house.

Llanwern 🎝

Llanwern means the church on marshy ground. It is a small village on the northerly edge of the Caldicot Levels, reclaimed from the sea by the Romans who built a sea wall and dug drainage ditches, which were known locally as reens. The monks from Goldcliff priory are reputed to have dug the large drainage ditch from Wentwood in the north to the Bristol Channel in the south, to combat flooding. This large reen is vitally important today and is maintained by the National Rivers Authority.

To the south of the village is the huge British Steel works from which the village is separated by the main London rail line. To the west a large and thriving golf course makes the division from Newport. To the north and east there is farmland interspersed with wooded areas and lovely pastoral views towards the high ground at Wentwood.

The church stands on the site of a much older church and is some distance from the heart of the village. It has recently had its peal of bells restored. In the churchyard is a large memorial to Lord Rhondda who owned much of the surrounding countryside and lived at Llanwern Park.

Lower Machen ❧

The traffic on the busy A468 from Newport to Caerphilly by-passes the small historical village of Lower Machen. Only a signpost acknowledges that a settlement exists behind the modern frontage of houses and large mature trees. But to visit the village is to enter into a timeless and peaceful world that defies the pace of the busy main road a few yards away.

Lower Machen was known purely as Machen until the village on the other side of the gorge, Upper Machen (mainly the product of the Industrial Revolution) grew up in the 18th and 19th centuries to supersede the older village in importance and size. Upper Machen eventually took over the sole name of Machen. But the Industrial Revolution came and went and now both villages are dormitories for people who work elsewhere, or, in the case of a large percentage of Lower Machen residents, a place for secluded retirement. Both settlements were further divided by the boundary changes that took place in 1974. Lower Machen is administered by Gwent, Machen by Mid Glamorgan.

The compactness of the village is deceptive for its importance was once widespread. Its boundaries stretched over the mountain and beyond. The Machen lordship in post-conquest times comprised approximately the present parishes of Abercarn, Machen, Bedwas, Bedwellty, Mynyddislwyn and parts of Henllys, Risca, Bassaleg and Panteg. But now, like Draethen nearby on the other side of the river Rhymney, it is mainly an estate village of 19th century construction built and administered by the great landowners, the Morgans of Tredegar. Yet its history still exists in the fallen walls of its own castle (Castell Meredydd), in the beautiful Elizabethan mansion (Plâs Machen) which was once the seat of the Morgan dynasty, and its close association with another castle – Ruperra.

Even further back in time there were Bronze Age settlements on the mountain above the village, evidence of which still remains, and on the plain by the river was a Roman settlement. When the present A468 road was constructed around Plâs Machen many Roman remains were discovered. For Lower Machen was once an important section of the imperial lead mines and also contained brickworks and iron forges run with slave labour. In the vestry of the village church, hidden by clergy vestments, is part of an old slab discovered in 1901. On the slab is a face which has huge staring eyes and a sunken square for a mouth. It has been identified as a Celtic-Romano gorgon. Ironically, this stone used in the building of the church turned out to be a pagan artefact!

The earliest surviving records of the church go back to 1102, although it may have been founded in the 7th or 8th century. Later it was used by the Morgan family who travelled to it from Ruperra Castle, which was the seat of the heir of Tredegar. Evidence of their involvement is on the tombstones in the churchyard and in the Morgan chapel to the right of the altar. The church is also famous for its many recently restored hatchments which line the walls. In the churchyard is the broken cross where in October 1741 Wesley preached a sermon in English. But the highlight of the church is its outstanding acoustics. Since 1968 the Lower Machen Festival has ensured that both players from around the world and an audience from near and far can share in this superb auditorium.

Machen's castle, Castell Meredydd, was built in the 11th century. It takes some finding and all that remains is the four foot high wall of a tower on a natural outcrop of limestone rock and the outline of a bailey. It was built by Meredydd the Terrible (hence its name) and was strategically important in that it guarded the entrance to the gorge that divides the flat coastal area from the hills and mountains of the inland area. In 1235 it was captured by the Normans which in turn signalled its downfall, until over the centuries its tumbled stones have become almost overlooked.

Plâs Machen, the Elizabethan manor house, was built in 1490 by Thomas Morgan, Esquire to the Body of Henry VII. But after Tredegar House was built it became a tenanted house and it lost a lot of its glories over the centuries. Today it is a farmhouse and a third of its original size, but even so it has 20 rooms and two families live inside its substantial walls. There is a rumour that an underground passage connects it to Ruperra Castle, but distance and terrain make this unlikely. It is best seen from the Draethen to Michaelstone road where its distinctive chimneys reach up from a bygone age.

The small tollhouse on the main road forms an unusual entrance to the village. It was probably built at the end of the 18th century. It is a condition that the owners of the modern house alongside maintain it. It has even been a Japanese tea house in recent years, having been acquired by an oriental enthusiast. Yet its original purpose was to collect tolls on the road from Newport to Caerphilly and, until the turnpikes were abolished in 1889, this was its function. But the tollhouse was also a home and several people in the vicinity had ancestors who were brought up in it. One such family was brought to ruin around 1822 when the tinworks in Upper Machen closed down and the toll revenue was drastically cut. The tollhouse keeper and his brother were jailed for debt and his pregnant wife died in the workhouse leaving nine children in the care of the parish.

Time has been kind to Lower Machen in that the A468 has taken the traffic away from it and Machen's larger settlement has absorbed much of what the 19th and 20th centuries have brought in their wake. Today Lower Machen provides a much needed interlude in a rushed modern world.

Marshfield 🦢

The parish of Marshfield lies on the Gwynllwg or Wentloog Levels almost halfway between Newport and Cardiff and although it might be assumed that the name derives from flat and marshy land, this is not so. The British rainfall table proves that less rain falls here than in both adjacent towns, owing to the fact that Marshfield has a chain of hills to the north and the sea to the south, both of which attract the rain clouds.

In the past, many of the inhabitants spoke Welsh and the village was known among the Welsh folk as Mairyn, which in its turn was a corruption of Ynys Mair or St Mary's Island, so called because the rising ground on which the church stands was surrounded on two sides by water, generally thought to be the Ebbw river. Gradually St Mary's Island became Mary's Field and then Marshfield.

Within the parish are two hamlets now almost merged into one but still retaining their separate names. Castleton or 'Cas bach' to the north and Blacktown. This name presents a mystery but one explanation is that after the flood of 1606 the persons drowned in the disaster were buried here. Hence, Blacktown. The land in this area is dissected by drainage channels known locally as reens. It is not known when they were originally executed but they were in existence in the Middle Ages.

There are two places of worship within the village and each has an interesting history. The original church dedicated to St Mary the Virgin was built in the reign of King Stephen (1135). There have been many changes over the centuries but the tower and the south entrance are original. Much restoration work was done in the 19th century and as recently as 1987 the interior walls were painted and the beautiful oak furniture repolished, a labour of love undertaken by church members.

The Davies family from Bryn Ivor Hall were Baptist supporters and they entertained the Rev Charles Haddon Spurgeon when he visited Castleton in 1859. This was the year that the present Baptist chapel was built at a cost of £2,000, and Spurgeon himself came to open it, his first visit to Wales. He was already a nationally renowned preacher, though he was then only 24 years of age. On the day of his visit around 5,000 people came by train, horseback or walked from miles around. A hay waggon was set up behind the institute for Spurgeon to preach from, the chapel not being large enough to accommodate the crowds.

The original chapel at Castleton was built in 1804, near to where the present bus shelter stands. Church and chapel members meet together on special occasions, particularly for the annual Women's World Day of Prayer, when the service is held alternately in church and chapel.

At the beginning of this century many young men of the village used to meet at a coffee house in Castleton for the purpose of reading and discussing the contents of various books. They called themselves the Young Men's Friendly Society. In 1923 Lord Tredegar made a gift of the ground and the money for the erection of a fine brick building for the use of these young men and it is still known as the YMFS Institute.

The village hall, built by Manpower Services in 1978, is at the other end of the village in Marshfield. Both these buildings are in daily use and provide facilities for meetings, concerts, annual fairs and fetes and are rented out for such occasions as wedding and birthday parties.

In the 1960s some ladies of the village got together and formed a group, calling themselves 'Young Wives', their main purpose to provide amenities for the old age pensioners. A little while afterwards the pensioners themselves formed their own over sixties club, but the Young Wives still provide them with a splendid Christmas dinner and summer tea complete with entertainment, and open the village hall every other Wednesday afternoon where they can enjoy a game of indoor bowls or cards or just a quiet chat over a friendly cup of tea. Incidentally, many of the original 'Young Wives' are now of pensionable age themselves. The money needed for these activities comes from weekly bingo sessions and their Autumn Fayre, which is a great attraction.

One inhabitant of whom the village is justifiably proud is an Olympic medalist. Lynn Davies (Lynn the Leap) won the Olympic

Gold Medal in Tokyo in 1964 in the men's long jump. He went on to win further gold medals in the Commonwealth Games in Kingston, Jamaica and the European Games in Budapest, both in 1966. Lynn captained the Welsh team and won another gold medal at the 1970 Commonwealth Games in Edinburgh and later that year was honoured by the people of Marshfield with the presentation of a set of Rumney pottery with his achievements and record inscribed in gold leaf. Lynn is still the holder of the British Long Jump record which was set 25 years ago in Berne, Switzerland.

Two firms have provided employment in the village. One is the Unigate Dairy opened just after the war when it was known as Cambrian United Dairies. It was rebuilt in 1983 when modern technology made many workers redundant. The other was the Ansells Brewery distribution depot, which operated in Marshfield for over 40 years until moving to Newport.

During the war, munitions were stored in Marshfield in reinforced concrete bunkers on the site where the depot now stands. These bunkers were used as offices until their recent demolition to make way for private housing.

Drivers, known as 'trunkers' would bring the beer from Birmingham for distribution to public houses in the area. One night, about 10.30 pm a driver alighting from his truck almost collided with a lady dressed in the uniform of a nurse with white cap and apron. He had turned to apologise when the apparition vanished. The tale is told that the experience so unnerved the man that he never again came to Marshfield.

One character of the past whom the older generation remember with affection was Ivor, who kept our streets free of litter. Every day he could be seen trailing around with his slow steady gait or eating his sandwiches in his little hut perched on spare ground at Groes Corner. On cold winter mornings when he lit his fire, he couldn't be seen for smoke. Now we have yellow litter bins and a mass of litter. Oh, for another Ivor to come along with his barrow and broom and pride in his work.

Many houses have been built in this area in the last 20 years with the consequent increase in population. People now commute to Newport or Cardiff and many travel over the Severn Bridge to Bristol and beyond to their place of work. Things are continually changing but there is still a wonderful community spirit in this village. Long may it continue.

Mathern 🐚

Nestling as it does near the river Severn, Mathern has for centuries been dominated by its church and bishop's palace. Agricultural in character, it is now slowly expanding and, together with the adjoining village of Pwllmeyric, is home to many residents who work in surrounding towns such as Newport, Cardiff and thanks to the Severn Bridge, as far afield as Bristol.

St Tewdric's church is still the spiritual centre of the village and services are held regularly each Sunday. The church magazine, which is run in conjunction with the other two churches in the group, helps to keep the inhabitants informed of local news and events.

The church was built in the 7th century. St Tewdric, to whom the church is dedicated, had been king of the Celtic kingdom of Morgannwg. In old age he became a hermit, but was called out of retirement to rally the kingdom's armies to fight the Saxons. Tewdric won the resulting battle but received a mortal axe-blow to the skull. Carried by his followers he was refreshed at the place which is now St Tewdric's Well and at his request the church was built near the spot where shortly afterwards he died. The well is maintained by the local council and many visitors come to the church and well each year.

Nearby is the bishop's palace, the former residence of the bishops of Llandaff (at least five bishops lie buried in St Tewdric's church and churchyard; the most famous of these was Bishop William Morgan, who completed the translation of the Bible into Welsh in 1588). The palace is now owned by British Steel who use it as a conference centre, and for important guests who stay there when visiting the steel works at Llanwern.

John Lee and Charles Pratt were great characters who lived in

110

the village. John Lee died, aged 103, in 1825 and is buried in the churchyard near the porch of St Tewdric's church. His tombstone bears the following inscription:

'John Lee is dead, that good old man.
We ne'er shall see him more.
He used to wear an old drab coat,
All buttoned down before.'

Charles Pratt, whose grave is nearby, was a great benefactor to the village and he left money and land to provide funds to teach the poor children of the village to read and write. Today the charity is still in existence and flourishes, mainly due to the fact that a private nursery school pays it a substantial rent each year. It is interesting to note that the village school, which was closed in 1988 and which was owned by Pratt's charity, was let to the county council at that time for a 'peppercorn' rent of approximately 75p per year.

In the parish is the mansion of Moynes Court, reputed to be the home of Thomas and Marjorie Moyne, who lived there in the middle of the 14th century. It is at present divided into apartments and the bottom end of the driveway is near the bridge carrying the M4 motorway which intersects the village.

The Vaughan-Hughes family until recently lived at the Wyelands, a lovely country house overlooking the village. Mr G.M. Vaughan-Hughes, who lived in the early part of this century, did much to stimulate the love of music in the parish and at that time the church possessed one of the best choirs in the district. Today the Mathern Ladies Choir carries on this tradition. The late Brigadier G.B. Vaughan-Hughes was also very much loved and respected and his passing was a great loss to the village.

Michaelston-y-Fedw 🌿

Michaelston-y-Fedw is a rather scattered village to the north of the A48 on the boundary of Gwent with South and Mid Glamorgan, in the green, unspoilt area between Newport and Cardiff. There is doubt as to whether the name means St Michael's by the birch tree (bedw being Welsh for birch) or that Fedw is derived from St Medwy, an early Welsh saint.

It is believed that parts of the church may be as early as the year AD 500, though the most important parts date from the 13th century. There was restoration work in the 15th century after a fire, when the tower was built to hold a peal of six bells. At this time also, the Kemeys Chapel was built by the Kemeys family, who lived in the mansion of Cefn Mably just across the county border until 1925. A more recent point of interest is the grave of Elizabeth Mackie, a local woman who was the first wife of Carl Hess, father of Rudolph Hess, the Nazi.

The old Roman road, the Via Julia which ran from Caerleon to Glamorgan, passes through the village about half a mile from the church. Near its route is Druidstone House which derives its name from what is said to be the oldest object in the village – the Druids' Stone – which is possibly a relic of a chambered long barrow.

The village school is no more. Originally endowed by a past rector, Benjamin Tate, it closed in 1969 because of the policy of closing small, uneconomic schools and children are now transported by bus to Marshfield school. It has become the village hall and the school house is a private dwelling.

There has never been a village shop and the post office closed after being run by the same family for several generations.

In the 1930s there was a regular bus service to Newport and for a few glorious years from about 1956 the Ebbw Vale to Cardiff bus ran through the country lanes every two hours both ways. However, it was withdrawn and there is an infrequent service from The Cefn Mably Arms, the local hostelry, to Cardiff. This is totally unsuitable for anyone going to work or for evenings out.

It means a half mile trek for many people, and it is two miles to a decent bus service on the Cardiff-Newport road. Michaelston-y-Fedw is not the place for a car-less family unless they are all capable of long-distance walking.

There was a Baptist chapel here from 1862 until 1967, when it was demolished. All that is left is the graveyard, and the remains of the old baptistry which was filled by damming a stream which still runs through the field known to the old inhabitants as 'The Tinkers'.

The river Rhymney forms the northern boundary with Mid Glamorgan and is crossed by two lovely old stone bridges which are unfortunately often abused by large vehicles. The river, not so long ago blackened by coal pollution from the mining valley, is now clean and well stocked with fish. As a result, the kingfisher is a very welcome resident. The road from the village to Castleton is called Heol-y-glo (Coal Lane) because it was used as a route for transporting coal.

In past years most people who lived here were employed by the Tredegar estate, local farms and Cefn Mably House, both as a private dwelling and later a sanatorium and geriatric hospital. The farms have been and still are very productive with grain, vegetables, dairy cattle and sheep. Things have changed lately, and we have been treated to a patchwork of brilliant yellow oil seed rape, golden corn, green cabbage and sky-blue linseed. There is a trout farm and a huge glasshouse growing tomatoes, which is not quite the blot on the landscape that was feared but looks from a distance like a lake. There may well be more change if plans for a very large golf course materialise; one of the main worries is the amount of traffic it would generate.

Almost all the area used to be owned by the Cefn Mably and Tredegar estates, but the farms and cottages were sold as the big estates ran down and they have been modernised and extended. Most people do not now work locally and have a wide variety of occupations. Many farms are unrecognisable now as the barns have all been converted to country houses. A small amount of new building has been allowed. The community council has discussed the possibility of asking Newport Borough to declare the village a conservation area. We hope we will remain a green, unspoilt area.

The Monmouthshire Canal (Fourteen Locks) ⚜

At exit 27 of the M4, the motorway passes over the Crumlin branch of the Monmouthshire Canal. The traveller who looks toward the rising ground will notice a flight of derelict locks. They seem insignificant from the motorway today, but at the end of the 18th century, when they were built, their construction was a major engineering triumph, and they became the centre of a community now gone.

The Fourteen Locks Canal Centre is well worth a visit. To find it, leave the M4 at exit 27 and the canal centre is just off the B4591 less than a mile away at High Cross. The facilities there are jointly managed by Gwent County Council and Newport Borough Council and include an interpretation centre, car park and picnic area, which has been laid out around the top lock and top 'pound'. The pond has been dredged and refilled. Now the still water reflects the silhouettes of the mature trees and there is a feeling of peace and tranquillity. It has not always been so, for in the mid 19th century barges carrying coal, timber and stone queued here awaiting their turn to enter the lock system. The remains of 14 locks have been preserved as an industrial archaeological site, and a waymarked trail explains how they worked and how side ponds were used to conserve water – a necessity when we consider that each lock held 40,000 gallons!

A walk through a site like this can fire the imagination of some people as they envisage life here in times past. Others need more help. The historical exhibition gives a great deal of information, but not that much about the life of the people; and it's people who really bring a place to life.

My great-grandfather and grandfather lived and worked at Fourteen Locks and my father grew up in the lock-keeper's cottage

114

which once stood opposite the interpretation centre – for his father was the last lock-keeper on this stretch of the canal. I have read the diary of the lock-keeper in great-grandfather's day, have heard old inhabitants talk about Sunday school outings on the barges in grandfather's day and been told stories by my father of life when he was a boy.

What a close-knit community it was in 1859. Lock-keeper Jones could have told you the exact times of many births and deaths, as well as full details of any weddings. He wrote these things down in his diary, together with who had gone to Newport market to buy pigs, and how much they paid for them; how he had warned boatmen for not strapping the lock-gates properly and so wasting water; and about the problems that arose when some old boats slipped on the mud and blocked the waterway. He wrote, too, about 14th May 1859, a day everyone at Fourteen Locks would always remember, for on that day young Phoebe Williams fell in the lock by the lock-keeper's house and drowned. Canal locks were, and still are, dangerous places.

Now, imagine a wintry scene on the canal bank at the end of January 1861. The waterway has been frozen hard and closed to traffic for a month. No trade means no money, so no one is very happy. At last the ice-boat, with its iron bow and strong towing horses, forces its way through and trade can commence again.

Winters did seem to be much harder then than now. The canal company ice-boat was needed practically every year to keep the canal open. It often had four horses pulling it, as well as plenty of men standing at the boat's bar to rock it. One day in February 1855 eight horses were needed to pull the ice-boat through. That year the ice was so strong that it cut holes right through two of the ordinary barges.

By the beginning of this century there was much less barge traffic, and one day in 1905 we find Messrs Jones and Roberts, who own most of the boats left, cleaning and scrubbing their working barges so that they can be used as pleasure craft. Bethesda Sunday school has paid £5 10s to hire four boats for their annual Whit Monday outing – a canal cruise to Risca and back. This happened most years and was always eagerly awaited.

115

On the Monday about 200 men, women and children lined up on the canal bank at the Cefn. They were all dressed in their best clothes. Ladies wore dresses and elaborate straw hats, while men donned suits and caps, or even bowler hats. The children looked like miniature adults. Up to 60 people crowded on to each barge. Although it was standing room only for many, this was the treat of the year. After the boat trip everyone went back to the chapel for tea and the family day out ended with games and races in the field.

The last picture is of a clean, well-maintained canal in 1913. The waterway is now of little economic importance and the local boys have made it their swimming pool during the summer holidays. Their favourite place is the wall at the end of the top lock, for this makes an ideal diving platform.

My father was one of those boys. He dived well and was more adventurous than most. Unfortunately, on one occasion he landed too near to the overflow weir and was sucked into the culvert. I can just imagine how frightened he was as the force of the water carried him through the narrow culvert and out into the side pond some considerable distance away.

As I walk around the now dry, but still elaborate, interconnected culverts, channels and side ponds at Fourteen Locks I realise how lucky my father was to live to tell me the tale.

Mounton 🌿

To the west of Chepstow, nestling between the A48 Chepstow to Newport road and the B4235 Chepstow to Usk road, lies the little hamlet of Mounton. It is the most peaceful place, so quiet and pretty, with the wood pigeons, crows and rooks cawing in the tall trees, and the sound of Mounton brook rippling below. It is hard to realise that Bristol, Newport and the M4 are so near, as few cars negotiate the narrow lanes. Today Mounton consists of eleven properties, most of them unrecognisable as the cottages that used to house Sir Edward Currie's estate workers.

The main feature of Mounton is St Andoenus' church. From

the outside the church looks quite plain, but inside it is a different matter. The church seats about 50. For lighting, the old chandeliers that used to hold candles have been converted to electric candle-lamps, as have the wall fittings, and with the stained glass windows it is both pretty in daylight and at night. There is no modern organ. Music is provided by a pedal harmonium which is very old.

'Mounton to me is a very special place. My mother was always talking about the years she spent there and said they were the happiest days of her life; although it must have been a very hard life in its own way. Everything in the way of food or household items had to be bought and carried from Chepstow as there was no transport; even today there is no public transport. There was no telephone anywhere near and if the doctor was needed someone had to go into Chepstow to fetch him. The nearest schools were either Mathern or St Arvans, which was why my parents moved from Mounton when I was nearing school age.

Mounton House overlooks the valley, although it cannot be seen from there because of the trees. It is now a special school, owned and run by the county council, and the children from the school often attend morning service at the church and play an active part in church events.

The Forestry Commission now looks after most of the woodland around Mounton, although in earlier days this was the estate's

Church of St Andoenus at Mouton

responsibility. My mother often used to tell me how she and my father used to sneak into the woods to gather wood although this was frowned on by the estate. The woods were kept for game and hunting and as a gamekeeper lived in the cottage below my parents', my father's job would have been at stake had they been caught. There were always plenty of rabbits around but the gamekeeper made sure no one took any. Once he actually shot a cat of ours when he saw it going into the woods as he said it was going after pheasant chicks he was rearing for shooting. However, my mother did once get the better of him by catching a trout from the brook with a piece of twine, a pin and a worm. It seems she tied this to a plank they used for crossing the brook, left it there overnight and to her surprise the next morning she had caught a trout.

Apart from the alterations to the houses, Mounton has changed little. The same old paths cross the fields from Pwllmeyric to the church and there are always blackberries and nuts to be picked in the autumn and walks in the wood.'

Nash ✣

Situated on the outskirts of Newport and bordered by the Bristol Channel, river Usk and the neighbouring villages of Goldcliff and Whitson, Nash was originally a farming village with other crafts relating to that industry. The name of the village is supposedly taken from an ash tree, of which there are many.

In 1893 East Usk Lighthouse was built and it has been tended by generations of the same family since that date. Thomas Williams, who lived at Fish House, dragged the steel used to build the lighthouse, with the help of his horse, from what is now the main road down the long lane to the coast. It is thought that is how he was given the task of looking after it. It was originally built on legs, but when sea defences were improved, was incorporated into the sea wall. Originally lit by twelve gas cylinders, which would last a year, it was converted to electricity in 1972. Local men used also to work regularly on the sea wall, but this is now the responsibility of the River Board and sadly at Nash acess to the sea wall is difficult.

The church at Nash as it stands today with its beautiful spire, dates probably from the 1500s when it was recorded that a new church was built from the old. However, a church stood on the site for many years before this. During the reign of Charles II, the Arney family gave to the parish a cottage and six acres of land for the support of the poor. The cottage is now the public house – The Waterloo Hotel, and the six acres is the field behind what was the local school. Both of these still belong to the parish, and the trust is administered by the community council to the benefit of all parishioners. The unusual features of the church are its three-tiered pulpit, box pews, minstrel gallery and leper squint.

The local school, as with many in rural communities, closed in spite of a valiant fight to keep it open, in 1981. Local children are bussed to schools outside the village and the school is now a private house.

The Second World War changed the face of Nash as a largely farming community, with the building of two artillery camps at Uskmouth and Pye Corner for the troops. These were occupied by the homeless after the war until council houses were built much later. Industry came in the form of Uskmouth power station which was started in 1948. It provided employment for many local men, as of course did the Llanwern steelworks at a much later date. Now with the motor car, people with many and varied occupations live in the village.

In 1976, after much hard work, the local community hall was opened. Today it is probably the centre of much of village life. It has regular dances and bingo, and provides the meeting place for mothers and toddlers and the WI. Many private functions are also held there. Each year a garden show, pet show and children's sports are held there, providing much local interest.

Currently Nash and neighbouring villages are under threat from the M4 relief road. Proposals are for a six-lane motorway to cut through the Gwent Levels virtually destroying life as we now know it.

Oakdale 🌿

'I consider it a privilege to have spent my childhood in a small mining village in Wales, albeit during strikes and the threat of the Second World War.

It was a classless society. We were all poor, but with the ignorance of childhood we were unaware of it. My parents cushioned us against the hardships. Nothing that might have worried us was discussed and I well remember the words "Not in front of the children" being used.

There were not many outings for us but a lot of love and a sense of security was ours. Honesty was instilled into us and sharing and unselfishness was taken for granted. At the dinner table, such was my mother's sense of "no favouritism" that she even counted the chips onto our plates. My grandmother often said that mealtimes with us were more entertaining than the pictures.

My life revolved around school and chapel. The seasons were punctuated by feasts and festivities.

Christmas meant dressing up warmly on Christmas Eve and carrying lanterns to visit local farms, where we sung carols and were invited into a warm kitchen for mince pies, made by the farmer's wife. There was always the Christmas party in the church hall. Mr Griffiths, a friend of my father always dressed up as Father Christmas. He played his part well and we never let on that we knew who it was.

New Year's Day would find us outside our local Italian ice cream shop awaiting the annual ritual when he would throw sweets and oranges to us. Of course the boys always got the lion's share. Inconceivably our kind Mr Conti was interned during the war years and we never saw him again.

St David's day began with the school eisteddfod and it was always my lot to recite, "This is the 1st March, on this day our patron saint was born," etc. We were rewarded by having a half day off school.

Palm Sunday meant chapel in the morning and always in our "best clothes" we trooped to Cwtyrbella churchyard to place flowers on family graves. I bitterly regretted that not one of my family was buried there. The insensibility of being a child!

Easter Sunday, after breakfast of coloured boiled eggs, it was to chapel again and then a walk to Penyfan pond, our local beauty spot. Halfway there we always stopped at the Cherry Tree Farm and hands cupped we partook of the delicious spring water.

Whitsunday brought the annual parade of the local chapel congregation through the village. This ended at the "rec" for the crowning of the Rose Queen. My sister was the Rose Queen one year. She was paraded around the village on the back of a lorry, decorated lavishly for the occasion. The lorry was preceded by our own brass band.

I was always in the scarf dance and maypole dance, dressed in mop-cap and long flowing dress. My partner for the maypole dance was always the same, best looking boy in the class and for years he was regarded as my "boyfriend". After all the high jinks we marched back to the chapel for a sumptuous tea party.

Summer days always seemed so full of sunshine and the days were long. We spent most of the school holidays in the nearby Ivy-bush, which was a large, dense wood full of wild flowers, shrubs and wild fruit bushes. We would leave home in the mornings and spend most of the day there partaking of wild fruit and edible plants. I think we must have learned to discern between edible and toxic plants from the older children. We did know the difference and no one ever suffered from our al fresco parties. With our friends we spent long hours in this wood, our parents knew we were safe and no harm ever came to us.

During August the Sunday school trip was a great event, our annual excursion to Barry Island. Ordered by our eldest sister we would pray for a "fine day tomorrow". It invariably was and very little sleep was had the night before the longed-for day.

One year my mother decided, during the winter months, to knit our bathing suits. We watched excitedly while each garment was completed. Came the big day and when we arrived in Barry Island, off came our clothes and on went our precious "bathers". Excitedly we ran into the sea and to our horror our suits didn't and hurriedly we pulled them up and went with great embarrassment to our parents. It was a disaster then but has given us much amusement over the years.

Lunch that day was always sandwiches and pop, a great treat because we were not allowed to drink this normally. Barry Island featured a long sandy beach and almost always there was a slight breeze. Over the years we must have consumed a great deal of that sand in our sandwiches. It was always a perfect day out. My father would take snaps of us and how we enjoyed the results of his developing these with curtains drawn in the bathroom. This was when the railways were at their peak and we were very well served by the GWR. A short walk to our local junction and we were away.

August seemed to go on for ever and we made full use of our freedom from school by amusing ourselves in various ways. The boys spent a lot of time in the river Sirhowy and although black from coal from the pit, nothing daunted, they swam whenever possible. We girls were above such things and indulged in games like hopscotch, whip and top, exchanging comics, etc. We especially enjoyed the afternoons when our father would take us to visit the pit ponies in the fields near our village. We would tempt them with sugar lumps and marvel at the fact that they would only see the daylight for this one week in the year.

A place very dear to my heart was our library. This was a mahogany-lined room in the Miners Institute. It was well endowed with old and new books and I loved just being there. It had its own smell and I spent lots of time there, happy to touch the books and choose which to take home. We were never censored in our reading. I was saddened when the Institute was dismantled brick by brick and is now being erected in St Fagans Welsh Museum.

Television was unheard of in my childhood. The radio was very important in our house. We enjoyed plays, series, especially comedy and all the music. Listening to the radio in our living room gave us a sense of togetherness.

It was in that living room as a child I sat and looked through the window, onto the long garden and contemplated my future. Years later, until my mother died and we lost the house, I would sit at that same window, looking onto that same long garden and contemplate my past.'

Panteg-New Inn 🦢

Today the village of Panteg-New Inn is a very extensive one, with a population of nearly 6,000. Although at least 300 years old, the name was bestowed in the late 19th century. Its spine is the main road from the old turnpike in the north to Lower New Inn in the south. From that main road numerous branches extend westwards as far as the Afon Lwyd and eastwards to Jerusalem Lane, and up Golf Road. The older inhabitants of New Inn have usually regarded the river as its western boundary and on crossing, one entered a sort of lonely 'no man's land' on the way to Griffithstown.

Two hundred years ago the picture was very different. Like the greater part of Monmouthshire the New Inn district was entirely rural. It included a few farms such as Clarewain and some very widely scattered dwellings plus the main settlement alongside the lane from the New Inn pub (today called the Lower New Inn) down through Pontyfelin to Pear Tree Cottage (where there was also a mill and buildings which housed a cider press). The latter lies alongside the former ford across the Afon Lwyd. Before the New Road was built a few years after the First World War, this ford was the only vehicle crossing of the river between the bridge at Pontymoel and Pontrhydyrun. Many of the houses on the highway opened up their front rooms as shops and sold all types of wares. Now we can proudly boast numerous shops of all kinds, a post office, a bank and a health centre.

At the top of Pontyfelin Lane the old nucleus of the village lay adjacent to the Lower New Inn at the junction with Newport Road. A common feature of many rural settlements in Britain was the grouping of inn, wheelwright, smithy and shop plus the church. At Lower New Inn were four of these features, with the Independent (Congregational) chapel only a field away substituting as it were for the Anglican church. However, St Mary's church, Panteg, was quite separate, almost a mile distant from the Lower New Inn. The vehicle approach to the church was from a point on Sluvad Road, thence southwards via the Glebe

St Mary's Church, Panteg

Cottage, now derelict. Today's Church Lane was made many years later. The origin of Panteg church is unknown but legend has it that it was given to St Cybi, a cousin of St David, by King Etelic of Edlogan. St Cybi flourished between AD 540 and 570. The church known as St Mary the Virgin, was completely rebuilt in 1849. Its tower has three bells (two of which are dated 1661).

New Inn occupied parts of two parishes separated by the brook which today rises near Greenlawn school, then flows between The Walk and Prospect Place, then behind The Teazer public house, and under the highway opposite the garage. South and east of that stream is the parish of Panteg, whilst north of it is the parish of Llanvihangel Pontymoel.

The Llandegfedd reservoir was built by the Cardiff Waterworks in 1966, and it is very popular for yachting, windsurfing, fishing, bird watching and nature trails. The beautiful setting makes it an ideal place for visitors to the area.

Many locals are employed at British Steel, Parke-Davies (Pharmaceutical Labs), ICI Fibres and Girlings who make component parts for brake systems.

The Institute was the recreational place for the local men, where they could play snooker and billiards. This was re-built in 1943 and renamed Panteg Public Hall. Many village activities are held here. New Inn holds a village fete in June, and St Mary's church have their fete in August. Both are very well supported. The polo grounds, once the site of many great fetes, is now an industrial site.

Cpl Edward Thomas Chapman, late of the Third Monmouthshire Regiment and a resident of New Inn, was awarded the Victoria Cross whilst serving in Germany on 2nd April 1945, for leading his patrol in the repulse of heavy odds, with total disregard for his own safety. He subsequently carried his wounded commanding officer back to their lines, in the process of which the latter was killed by a wound in the head, shot by a sniper. The bullet grazed Cpl Chapman's hip. Cpl Chapman was also awarded the British Empire Medal, running cross country for his regiment, whilst serving in the Suez Canal crisis with the Territorial Army. The citation is on display at Brecon Museum.

The Bush Inn, Penallt

Penallt ✣

Penallt lies south of Monmouth, 700 feet or so above sea-level on the west bank of the river Wye. Penallt means top or head of the hill. It covers an area of three square miles consisting of several hamlets.

Employment in years gone by was chiefly on or connected to the land. There were many farms of comparatively small acreage rearing cattle, sheep and pigs and with many cider apple and perry pear orchards. The plentiful stone, particularly the 'pudding' or 'jack' stone provided raw material for making millstones which were then manoeuvred down the steep slopes to the Wye and conveyed by barge to their final destinations. Many Penallters were employed at the Redbrook tinplate works and would cross the river by ferry to work.

Nowadays, a fairly high proportion of the population commute to work. Penallt is still a largely farming community but incomes are supplemented by diversification. Christmas and Easter bring feverish activity at Penygarn farm with a team of local ladies helping prepare turkeys and chickens for the trade. At Springfield Farm Jack and Jean Evans run a milk round and have a caravan site. A fishing syndicate use the trout lake developed from the stream beside the house. Cdr Tony Collett, who had a beautiful garden on Lydart and was a famous orchid breeder, inspired Eileen Williams at nearby Quarry Farm to take up flower arranging. She has become a great expert in this field and a winner of many prizes at the county shows and further afield.

The beautiful and peaceful surroundings have inspired the artistic world. Bernard Shaw was a frequent guest of Sidney and Beatrice Webb at The Argoed and is said to have written some of his plays whilst staying there. Sidney Webb helped to found the London School of Economics and the Fabian Society. Walter Keeler lives in the village and is a potter of international renown specialising in salt-glazed stoneware.

Peter Scourse and his talented artist wife keep and train hunting hawks. Their knowledge of these birds has led to their cottage becoming a hospital for the many casualties referred to them by local vets and the public. There are also several very talented amateur as well as professional artists in Penallt. The fruits of their labours are sometimes to be found at the annual fete or other fundraising events. Here too may be found the products of the many excellent cooks in the village. The Harvest Supper held at Pelham Hall is an eagerly awaited event when a high proportion of the village gather to enjoy outstanding local fare. Over the years at such events, Jimmy Saunders of the Limekilns is a top priority guest if anything is to be auctioned. His inimitable repartee is guaranteed to bring howls of mirth and rash spending of funds. Who else could persuade a normally thrifty population to part with £7 for a packet of tea, for instance?

Dr Stephanie Tyler, Conservation Officer for Wales for the Royal Society for the Protection of Birds and well known for her broadcasts, is also a village resident. She took a great interest in the Pentwyn Farm project – a property situated near The Bush Inn. It featured in the media in 1990/91 when Gwent Wildlife Trust ran a successful national campaign to raise funds to purchase this unique haven of wildlife with its agriculturally unimproved pasturelands. The cottage has been restored and the pastures preserved for future generations to enjoy.

There are many retired people who now live in Penallt and enjoy the tranquillity of the surroundings. The old troughs and millstones that once ground the corn or crushed the cider apples now grace many local gardens.

The school sadly no longer rings with children's laughter – the youngsters go to the modern school at Trellech. St Mary's church, built in Victorian times as a school chapel and as a chapel of ease for parishioners who found the mile trek to the Old Church too much, is being used nowadays for small village events as well as for services.

Recreation is well provided for in the village. The Bush Inn with its glorious views over the Wye to Gloucestershire is beside the village green where Penallt Morris Men (formed by our present vicar) dance on May Day and at other times throughout the year to give a colourful and nostalgic air to the scene. The Boat Inn at the bottom of Lone Lane provides refreshment for walkers or canoeists and entertainment for lovers of folk music and jazz.

Many of the ancient footpaths have been reopened and finger-posted over the past few years making it easier to enjoy the many special views and perhaps glimpse the more secretive wildlife such as deer, badgers and foxes which abound in Penallt.

Pelham Hall, built originally in 1923 and host to many a memorable village function in the past, was rebuilt and enlarged to form a new hall and sports complex in 1992. Alongside the hall is the thriving tennis club formed in 1978 on land generously provided by the Hartleys of Moorcroft House. A cricket club existed at Moorcroft during the 1890s and, up to the outbreak of the Second World War when the house was occupied by the

Hon Arthur Pelham. The Hartleys made land available once more in 1982 for a cricket pitch and the club now has its own ground alongside the new Pelham Hall.

Pigeon racing was a sport enjoyed in the past. Beekeeping is a hobby pursued by many Penalltrs today; the plentiful trees and flowers must be a bee's paradise! Horse riding has always been a very popular activity. More recently hot air balloons may be seen rising up above the trees as they take off from a centre near the Old Church.

Ty Mawr convent at Lydart was founded in 1929 by the Society of the Sacred Cross. Twelve guests can be accommodated and the convent is largely self sufficient with its own small farm and vegetable and fruit gardens. It has given a sense of tranquillity to visitors from all over the world.

No one should leave Penallt until they have visited the Old Church, situated a mile from the modern village. Follow the fingerposts and look out for the base of an old stone cross under a large chestnut tree where the footpath emerges at Cross Vermond. Here, pallbearers would rest the coffin and sing a psalm after the steep haul out of the Blackbrook valley. If you marry at the Old Church, you may be 'roped' on the narrow lane from the church as you leave after the service. Local children hold a rope across the road as the bridal pair approach and the groom must throw his small change to the children to allow onward passage. The Old Church is an architectural gem originating from about the 12th century. It has a saddleback tower and many historic features. Set high above the Wye it commands one of the best views of the valley. What a wonderful resting place at the end of your days.

Penhow 🐝

Penhow is a small village midway between the towns of Newport and Chepstow, four miles north of the Bristol Channel on the southern slopes of a ridge of high ground rising to 989 feet. It covers an area of 1,843 acres, most of which is agricultural land, the higher ground being used for forestry. In 1801 at the time of the first national census the population was 138, rising to approximately 400 in 1956 and 800 in 1993.

Before the M4 motorway was built, the road passing through Penhow was the main South Wales to London road and was first mentioned in records in 1798 during the reign of George III – in an act of Parliament which was passed for the repair of the road from Newport, through Penhow.

Today Penhow has a pleasant mix of old and new properties providing a peaceful, semi-rural environment for its inhabitants. Amenities include two general stores, one of which incorporates a post office, and a public house – The Groeswen. There are two churches in the village – the Baptist chapel and the church of St John the Baptist, alongside which is Penhow Castle. St John's church hall, which is used extensively for local activities, was built and furnished in 1913 by the generosity of a local benefactress, Mrs Perry-Herrick, who died in 1915 – the family owned much of the land and property in Penhow at the turn of the century. The Hall was extended and modernised in 1984 with the help of the Manpower Services, paid for by Newport Borough Council, and was visited by the Mayor in May 1985.

The Baptist chapel was built early in the century to commemorate the centenary of the Bethany Baptist church, Llanvaches and was completed in 1911. In 1991 the chapel was extended by the addition of the Revd Henson Memorial Hall, giving extra space for meetings and social events.

The church of St John the Baptist is of Norman origin and was extensively restored in 1913. The choir and clergy stalls were made by the local carpenter from oak timber from the roof of the old tower. On the east side of the church there is a wooden cross that was brought back from Egypt from the grave of Trevor James, the only Penhow man to be killed in the 1914–18 war. There is also a fine peal of bells, and ringers come from far and wide to practise their art of 'ringing'. The church has many other interesting features and is well worth a visit, as also is Penhow Castle adjoining the church.

The castle is one of the oldest buildings still standing in Penhow, the most ancient part being a rectangular tower of the 12th century with a projecting parapet. The castle has been occupied over the centuries by several noble and farming families. The part of Penhow known as 'Parc Seymour' derived its name from one of the owners, William de St Maur, a Norman baron, whose family name was changed to Seymour. In recent years the castle has passed into the ownership of Mr Stephen Weeks who has spent much time and effort on restoration; this has resulted in increasing numbers of people visiting during the summer months.

There has never been a school in the village, the local children attending Langstone primary school, which is a few miles along the main road towards Newport. Secondary schools are within easy travelling distance in Newport, Caerleon, Caldicot and Chepstow. Until about 1960 children started their education at either Llandevaud or The Pike school at St Brides Netherwent. A children's rhyme went something like this:

'Llandevaud Bulldogs,
Pike School Cats;
If you see a Penhow child,
Please raise your hats.'

No doubt, there were at least two amendments!

Many activities take place in the village, the Women's Institute being just one of them. During the Second World War both the local WI and WVS worked tirelessly to help the community by collecting for the Red Cross etc; augmenting the national larder by preserving and canning fruit and making 2,000 lbs of jam!

In summary, Penhow is a village well located for access to both town and countryside: it is within easy reach of Newport, Cardiff and Bristol (via the Severn Bridge), as well as the smaller towns of Chepstow, Usk, Caerleon and Monmouth, to name but a few. It is surrounded by the most beautiful countryside of the Wentwood Forest, the Wye Valley National Park and the Usk Valley – and its inhabitants are indeed most fortunate to have the best of both worlds.

Peterstone Wentloog 🦢

The village of Peterstone lies on the Wentloog Levels halfway between Newport and Cardiff on the coast road stretching from St Brides to Rumney. The area is known as 'Little Holland'.

The lovely Norman church of St Peter, often referred to as the 'Cathedral of the Moors', bears a floodmark of 1606, when many lives of inhabitants and livestock were lost. It is recorded that over 1,000 people drowned and were buried in a communal grave in Rumney, then called Rompney. Long and hard hours were toiled on the soil for the next 20 years to bring the land into production again.

The small village school which comprised one room with a lobby and toilets down the backyard, used to take pupils from the adjoining village of Marshfield, using a footpath crossing the main South Wales railway line. Later many pupils passed to higher education due to the standard of teaching by the late Miss LM Harris. The school was demolished and the site used for a car park for the Six Bells Inn, when it extended its premises. The old inn was once thatched with a cottage each end and a mounting block in the centre.

Hephzibah Baptist chapel and two cottages were demolished for six houses to be built. The baptistry was included in one of the front gardens and has been converted into a fish pond. In the old days baptism used to take place in a reen near The Gout Farm, where there is now an 18 hole golf course and hotel.

The only means of public transport was the train from the station at Marshfield, so it was quite a distance to travel by trap, bicycle or Shanks's pony, especially in inclement weather! The fare to Cardiff was tenpence.

So many changes have taken place, when years ago every farmstead and cottage had pigs and poultry running free. Who cared about a cock crowing! In winter a pig would be killed and cured for bacon to provide good meals for the family, and a bowl of lard for pastry or to fry pancakes on a frosty afternoon. In the old days residents knew one another, but sadly today many newcomers commute and do not take part in village life.

Ponthir & Llanfrechfa ✣

The village of Ponthir (from the Welsh for long bridge) takes its name from the bridge straddling the Afon Lwyd. There are claims that the Roman legion at Caerleon built the first bridge to march troops and families to a hill camp at Candwr Lane in times of danger. It was still a wooden structure in 1600 when a Llanfrechfa yeoman left three shillings and fourpence in his will for its repair. At the time of the bequest Welsh was the language of the area. Records in 1677 show Ponthir in the lordship of Usk and manor of Edlogan.

The parish church was and still is All Saints Llanfrechfa. A church has been there since the 9th century. The porch dates from around then; the tower and carved roof from the 14th century. It was extensively rebuilt with over £4,000 raised and the renovated church consecrated on 1st September 1874. Llanfrechfa is reputed to derive its name from the Welsh St Brechfa.

The two villages have always shared many amenities. The local school was located at Llanfrechfa from the mid 19th century until replaced by a new church school built on a pleasant green field site at Ponthir in recent years.

During the Industrial Revolution, the area changed. The tinworks came in 1747 and provided local employment until 1920. The manager lived in a beautiful Tudor mansion opposite the present Tycerbyd (Coach House) which was the stables and coach house of the mansion. The tinmasters were mainly English and nonconformist. There was a growing nonconformist following using Gilwern Farm for services. The chapel at Caerleon used Welsh language only. In 1800 the tinmasters helped build Sion Baptist church, Ponthir, where services were held in English and Welsh. There is still a healthy congregation at Sion and they have raised money in recent years to refurbish the chapel. Services today are exclusively English, currently the dominant language of the area. The chapel is now a listed building. A manse was built by a local farmer when his daughter married the then minister, Rev Rees Griffiths.

All Saints, Llanfrechfa – celebrated its centenary in 1974

The tramroad came about this time bringing iron from Blaenafon to be shipped from Caerleon down the Usk to Bristol; there was no dock at Newport. There are still tram lanes at Llanfrechfa and Ponthir. Licences were granted to families to allow them to serve home-brewed ale and plain food to the tramroad workers while they waited on the tide for loading. There were eight inns in about a mile from The Crown, Llanfrechfa to the Ponthir Inn which is still a popular place for refreshment some 300 years on. A local legend has it that a horseman won a wager for riding his mount over the still steeply-pitched roof of the Ponthir Inn. Most of these inns have now reverted to private dwellings.

The railway was constructed on the site of the old tramroad. Ponthir station was opened with great ceremony in 1878 and much widened the horizons of the inhabitants of the area. The railway remains but, alas, the station closed in 1963 just as the population boomed.

The rifle range was built in 1905 by volunteers, with materials supplied by a local gentleman, on land rented by a farmer for two shillings and sixpence a year. The club was affiliated to the Welsh Rifle Club and was soon winning gold and silver medals all over the country. In 1923 heavy storms damaged the building, leading to its rapid demise. Funds in hand helped towards the construction of a new hall which later became the church hall and a community meeting place until the new hall was built at Ponthir on land donated by the Griffiths family, former residents of The Hafod. The hall is in constant use and the activities are many and varied.

Both villages are today primarily dormitory areas with the occupants reliant on car ownership and engaged in a variety of occupations. They form a caring community with old and new residents well integrated.

The new sports club has grounds adjacent to the new school and gives the cricket club a permanent home after nearly 100 years on sites at various farms.

Interesting local characters have included a farmer who used his tractor both to deliver coal and take his wife for shopping in Newport, and an innkeeper who kept a monkey with a penchant for stealing customers' caps.

Pontllanfraith 🐾

Situated in the Sirhowy valley, Pontllanfraith, with a population of 9,000, is only 18 miles north of Cardiff and twelve miles north west of Newport.

In 1850 Pontllanfraith was known as 'Tredegar Junction' but delving into the archives it is found that the English translation for Pontllanfraith is 'the bridge of the speckled church', because the sun shining on the Sirhowy river cast a speckled effect on the water which, in turn, reflected on a bridge near a church.

The main occupation of Pontllanfraith, in earlier years, was farming but when the coal mines were sunk in the vicinity, mining was introduced.

Gelligroes Mill (at a sunken crossroad of uncertain date) was used for grinding corn, and over 50 years ago the output of the mill depended upon the amount of grain the farmers brought along to a Mr Moore, the miller of that period. Mr Moore introduced 'wireless' to the area before the First World War, and on one occasion this gentleman received a message, on his primitive apparatus, that a ship was in distress. It turned out to be the sinking of the *Titanic* in 1912. The mill has recently reopened as a corn and flour mill. The cottages alongside are now a candlemaking workshop, and Blackwood Amateur Radio enthusiasts are establishing a radio museum in the old mill.

Islwyn, a poet of great esteem, wrote his poem *The Nightingale* within the sound of the mill.

Tradition has it that early Christians here began to build their first church overlooking a grove where pagan ceremonies were held. The building mysteriously collapsed, on two occasions, at night. In the darkness a voice said, 'Myned-is-llwyn' ('Go below the bush'). Heeding this celestial command, the unhallowed spot was left and the church was built in its present position.

The first Elim chapel was built in 1869 at a cost of £100 17s 8d. There was an open fire and paraffin oil lamps were fixed on the walls. Because of the lack of facilities, the nearby stream, in Islwyn Terrace, was used for regular baptism. When the present Elim

The mill at Gelligroes

chapel was built in 1912 (by William Williams and sons) the old chapel was used as a bakery. The cost of the new building was £500.

Pontllanfraith Technical Institute and school was the first of its kind in Wales. It is situated on Sir Ivors Road, and is now a flourishing youth centre. The main venues of education are the junior, infants, comprehensive and Penllwyn schools. Further education, with numerous classes to suit all tastes and talents, is readily available at Pontllanfraith leisure centre.

The civic centre (Islwyn Borough Council offices) and the health centre are imposing buildings. They are extremely busy places, well maintained, and are a credit to the authorities.

The Penllwyn Hotel (Penllwyn Mawr manor house) is now surrounded by housing estates, and these estates have a panoramic view of the Sirhowy valley. The manor house came into being soon after the Wars of the Roses, and because of its architectural importance the exterior of the building has to be maintained in its original form.

There were two railway stations in Pontllanfraith, the LMS and GWR (high and low levels), and at one time, Sir Julian Hodge was employed as a booking clerk. The late Edgar Phillips (Trefin Archdruid Gorsedd of Bards) was a Welsh master at the grammar school.

The first man to receive the Freedom of the Borough was the late Sir Harold Finch (MP for Bedwellty). Sir Harold made his home in Pontllanfraith when he married in 1922. The Rt Hon Neil Kinnock (MP for Islwyn) has a second home in Sir Ivors Road and he is frequently seen in Pontllanfraith and the neighbouring town of Blackwood.

A ghost and a poltergeist are said to dwell within a mile of Pontllanfraith. A public house called The Three Horseshoes in Pentwynmawr was the home to a poltergeist which was very active around the year 1924. Ornaments dropped from their shelves, of their own accord, pictures 'took wing' and knives and forks often danced a jig. The poltergeist ceased to be active when the landlord of that time died, following a short illness.

Aunty Polly Cummings, however, is still around to this day.

She was a past landlady of the Cross Oaks Inn, at Penmain. She makes her presence known when electric lights and alarm systems suddenly become inoperative, for no apparent reason. Kettles move unaided, and a soft breeze is often felt. Aunty Polly Cummings's activities do not deter anyone. They only enhance the mystery of the Cross Oaks Inn.

A new bypass road is now under construction near the historical Gelligroes mill. When the road is completed it will be possible to travel from Newbridge to Caerphilly, in a lesser time.

Today, Pontllanfraith comprises small factory complexes, shops, garages, a sub post office and a large supermarket.

Pontnewynydd 🦢

In the mid 1730s a young married couple named Edmund and Mary Jones came over the mountain from the other valley to live in Pontnewynydd. He was a preacher and later became known as the prophet because he predicted a number of future events which did actually happen. At that time there were very few houses in Pontnewynydd but he held services in the open air outside his cottage. He decided in 1740 to build a chapel in the fields opposite his cottage and a piece of land was purchased for twelvepence halfpenny for this purpose. The couple gave their savings of £30 towards this building and eventually the chapel was built and Edmund Jones named it Ebeneezer, saying this would be the name of his successor – which in fact was correct.

In time three coal mines were sunk just a few miles from Ebeneezer – Blaenserchan, Llanerch and Tirpentwys. A tin plate forge was established just some 200 yards away from the chapel and, of course, a large number of houses were built.

Today the mines and the forge have disappeared but Ebeneezer still stands. It stands in the middle of a graveyard with Edmund and Mary Jones's grave just a few yards from the front door. It is not an attractive building from the outside but once you walk through the vestibule you will find a beautiful chapel of unusual design and with a rather special atmosphere.

Eventually one of Edmund Jones's assistant pastors left Pontnewynydd and sailed with others to America where in Pennsylvania they established a small settlement which they named Ebensburg and occasionally some of their descendants come over and pay a visit to Ebeneezer chapel in Pontnewynydd.

Portskewett & Sudbrook

Situated on the Severn estuary between the existing Severn crossing and the new bridge under construction, Portskewett – together with Sudbrook – is an ancient and important site. Human remains found there date back to megalithic times, well before the Celtic Silurian tribe ruled the area.

Giraldus Cambrensis (Gerallt Cymro) in his book *Journey Through Wales* in 1188 describes the country north to south from the river Gwdir in Anglesey to Portskewett in Gwent.

The name Portskewett derives either from Porth Ysgewydd – port of the elder wood, or Porthiscoed – port of the lower wood, the latter being now more generally accepted.

In the Welsh Triads, Portskewett is named as one of the three main ports of Wales in medieval times. The river crossing was very important and was mentioned in records in 1645. In the 18th century a regular ferry service was established which was in use until the building of the Severn Tunnel railway crossing. All over Gwent old milestones directed coaches and travellers to the New Passage Ferry. John Wesley was one such traveller, staying at Black Rock Hotel before 'mounting his pony and riding into Wales'. Black Rock picnic site is all that remains of Black Rock House. This was the ferry hotel providing food and shelter for the travellers; the dining room held 100. It was finally demolished in 1970.

Sudbrook, already an ancient site, developed with the building of the Severn railway tunnel. This started in 1877 and was opened in 1886. The previous attempt at building a tunnel failed. Lives were lost from flooding caused by a hidden freshwater spring, the source of which is still unknown. Millions of gallons of water from this spring are pumped out daily and used locally. Without this effort the tunnel could not be used.

The tunnel builder, Thomas Walker, built a self-contained village for his workers at Sudbrook including a post office, shop, hospital, school and chapel.

There are many sites and some buildings of interest in Portskewett. The megalithic burial at Heston Brake is in a field alongside the church. It is a mound said to be the site of the palace of the kings of Gwent, and the hunting lodge of King Harold of Wessex. In Celtic history it is where the Romans eventually captured Caradog (Caractacus), Celtic leader of opposition to Rome.

There are Roman remains around the area but the church of St Mary is the oldest building in Portskewett, being mainly Norman, while the old rectory is late 17th/early 18th century.

The Manor Farm at the crossroads must be the oldest habitation in Portskewett. Tudor in origin – possibly even older, the 17th century addition has a Restoration plaster ceiling in the lounge, and on the gable exterior end three cartouche arms with fleur de lys. These are believed to commemorate the visits of Charles I during the Civil War when he used the Black Rock crossing.

South Farm on the road to Sudbrook has parts dating back to the 17th century. Portskewett House is Victorian and belonged to the Lysart family, of industrial importance in Newport.

Between the wars houses around Portskewett, together with some land, were rented to miners suffering from illness as a result of their work. They were, and still are, called 'the settlements'. One of them has the most beautiful summer garden of bedding plants and is visited by many people.

Sudbrook, too, has sites of interest. The second century BC Iron Age-Celtic promontory fort is well worth a visit. Here in the 1st century AD took place the last big battle between the Celtic Silures and the Romans.

There is also a ruined church and, although underground, the Severn Tunnel is itself marked above ground by its large pump-house.

Portskewett inhabitants lead very busy social lives, from the very youngest in the mother and toddler group to 80 year olds in the Mothers' Union. We have a mini-rugby group, Scouts, a youth club, Women's Institute, the over forties club, an over sixties group called the Good Companions and whist drives. There are numerous outings throughout the year, some all day and some evenings only. There are special 'evening do's', Christmas parties, birthday parties, bazaars, folk dances and discos. We also have two fetes; the church fete and the village and carnival fete.

The local pub plays its part in the social life of the village too. It serves excellent food and from time to time it holds special evenings.

In the local park the Model Car Club has a racing track. Bowls, skittles, golf, fishing, football and rugby facilities are all available within a few miles; also swimming, badminton, etc at the leisure centre in Caldicot about a mile away.

Local employment is catered for by Mitel, a telecommunications firm, and by a small industrial estate. Sudbrook has a large paper mill and the pumping station which stops the Severn Tunnel from flooding. We also have a post office and shop, a hairdresser's, several nurseries and a garage.

Raglan ⚜

The village of Raglan, known as 'Ragland' in medieval times, is dominated by its impressive castle and has grown where the main route from the Midlands divides to Abergavenny and Newport. The population has trebled since 1965 to the present figure of approximately 1,800, but it still retains its friendly village atmosphere.

In summer, colourful floral window boxes and hanging baskets decorate the centre of the village, which has won the Best Kept Village title several times and the Wales in Bloom competition in 1992. The High Street has a good selection of shops supplying all needs from ironmongery to ladies' and gent's clothing. There are also three pubs, a post office, junior and infants schools, a playgroup and a modern health centre. The village is served by an Anglican church and a Baptist church. Children travel to Monmouth for secondary education.

On a hill overlooking the village stand the remains of the 15th century castle. It was at the height of its grandeur when the Civil War commenced, but, after a ten week siege led by Sir Thomas Fairfax for the Parliamentarians, capitulated on 19th August 1646. The buildings were 'slighted' under the orders of Cromwell, and for a century the castle provided free building materials for the whole neighbourhood. Now maintained by CADW, the castle's hereditary keeper remains the present Duke of Beaufort. It is open daily to the public, and the grounds are sometimes used for theatrical events. It was in the great tower that early experiments of the first practical steam engine were said to have been carried out by Edward Somerset, the second Marquess of Worcester.

St Cadoc's church, in the centre of the village, was founded in the 14th century, and is well worth a visit. In the Beaufort chapel the north window is a striking testimony to the first Lord Raglan, who died in the Crimea in 1855. He had been Wellington's military secretary and lost an arm at the battle of Waterloo. The Raglan overcoat, with its special sleeve, was named after the first Lord Raglan.

Raglan Castle

In about 1860 a Miss Anna Marie Bosanquet gave a peal of bells to the parish, but later, having considered them too noisy sent them over to Llandenny church, some two miles away. However, in 1953, the church was presented with a peal of electronic bells, the first of its kind to be installed in a church in this country. Miss Bosanquet also donated the church tower clock in 1863, which observant passers by will notice has only three faces. This is because the railway, opened three years earlier, had incurred her displeasure, so she decreed that the station should be punished by not having a clock face in that direction. The present vicar of Raglan also serves the parishes of Bryngwyn and Llandenny.

Just below the church on Chepstow Road stands the old school built in 1857 by the Duke of Beaufort, who owned most of the land around Raglan at that time. This building, together with the junior school, now forms the Raglan community centre and is, amongst other things, used for community education classes.

A well known village character, Mr Ernie Morgan, has the distinction of being Raglan's first Honorary Citizen. He was awarded the MBE soon after his ninetieth birthday in recognition of his long and dedicated service to St Cadoc's church where he has been verger and sexton for some 50 years. A reflection of the village's conviviality was apparent when over 200 people attended his surprise ninetieth birthday party. Mr Morgan, the village's oldest born resident, has accumulated a wealth of memories of village life, which he has recorded on tape.

The attractive Baptist church was built in 1865 although the Baptist cause in Raglan was established nearly 50 years earlier, in 1818. The first little chapel on the opposite side of the road was for many years used both as a day school and Sunday school, the minister acting as schoolmaster. This building has now been turned into a dwelling house. The former manse, recently altered and renamed the Fellowship Centre, is now used by the Sunday school and as a meeting place for various groups such as the Women's Institute.

The village has several historic inns. The Beaufort Arms Hotel was once a coaching inn and probably dates back to Tudor times. The Ship Inn (formerly called the Sheep Inn) has a cobbled area to the front where sheep sales were held in by-gone days and on the cobbles stands a pump where villagers probably exchanged news whilst collecting their water for the day. The nearby Crown Inn is mainly 19th century although some parts are much older. The upstairs club-room is the meeting place for a number of clubs including the successful Young Farmers' Club which boasts over 60 members. Also in the High Street can be found the old courthouse, a magistrates' court until 1974.

There is an active sports and social life within the village with many thriving organisations catering for all age groups ranging from Beavers, Cub Scouts and Brownies to the Village Produce Association and Local History Group. The community spirit is further illustrated by the well supported 'Fun Run' in aid of a national charity which has been organised for the past ten years.

Basically a rural community, Raglan has seen a number of specialist commercial and service businesses grow in the vicinity recently, some of which are housed in a new enterprise centre of workshop units renovated from an old Land Army hostel built for land girls during the last war.

Rhiwderin

Travelling the road between Bassaleg and Machen alongside the old Brecon and Merthyr railway line (which ran from Newport to Brecon), turn right at the Rhiwderin Inn. The modernised station house is on your right as you drive over the level crossing or walk under the old archway and come into the centre of the village. Tredegar Street is facing you, and close at hand are the Tabernacle chapel, the old school (now the community centre), the village hall, the post office and shop.

All these buildings play an important part in the present day life of the village. The immaculately kept chapel has a loyal congregation and large Sunday school. The community centre is home to such activities as the Welsh nursery school, bowling club, dancing class, army cadets, karate and swimming clubs, and sees social occasions such as the St David's Day celebrations. The village hall was originally given to Rhiwderin by Lord Tredegar and was known as the 'library' with its books and papers, and later a billiard table was added. Now modernised it is home for the Women's Institute, Pensioners' Club, whist drives, Guides etc.

To the right of the Tabernacle is the Glochwen (White Bell) farmhouse, parts of which are reputed to have been built in the 17th century, and this is the oldest building in the village.

Years ago people travelled by train from Newport, walked along Pentre Tai Road (the village of houses) and climbed fields on the left to picnic in Foxwood where there were several cottages; in one it was possible to get teas, in another Mrs Bowen, a tailoress, trained some of the local girls. In this area there used to be a row of nailmakers' cottages. Nails were made at Tydu on the other side of the river Ebbw.

In the middle of the 19th century, the tinplate works arrived (managed by Robert Nurse), the station was opened, the houses in Tredegar Street were built – and also a bridge over the river Ebbw which inspired Gwilym Maesaleg to pen the following verse:

'The rapid river Ebbw
That flows so very free
It shall divide for ever
Rhiwderin and Tydu.
The peaceful population
That live on either side
They wanted some construction
To cross the Ebbw tide.
The noble ancient Ebbw
Of course one cannot blame
For rolling down the hollow
It always did the same.

Some able man selected
This object to disperse
The President appointed
Was worthy Robert Nurse.
The bridge was well erected

And well and truly trod
The contract was completed
Indeed by Thomas Dodd.
To benefit the future
The thoroughfare is free
Old Ebbw cannot sever
Rhiwderin from Tydu.'

The tinworks went into liquidation in 1878 and the site was taken over by the Tredegar estate as a yard, and also by Periams brush factory.

Prior to the First World War, Rhiwderin band led the annual carnival in aid of the Royal Gwent Hospital (then entirely voluntary). There was also a football team which won the, then famous, Woodstock Cup. The local MP Sir Leoline Forestier Walker took a keen interest in the team and used to arrive, from Westminster, at Rhiwderin station, to be met by the family dogcart and taken to the local pitch. During the First World War this team assembled at the bottom of Tredegar Street before joining up 'en bloc' in Newport. Although the team was revived after the war it disappeared in the 1920s, when the Rhiwderin Male Voice Choir came into evidence for many years.

In 1927 classrooms at the school were taken over for secondary school pupils and in 1929 four more classes were started in the chapel. This continued until 1935 when Bassaleg school opened.

Today this is an active and friendly village. Occupations of the residents are many and varied and although horseriders are frequently seen in the area, the car is the predominant form of transport, leaving the old Brecon and Merthyr line to carry only goods through Rhiwderin.

Rogerstone

Rogerstone lies on the edge of the coastal plain in the approaches to the Western and Sirhowy valleys; three and a half miles from both Newport and Risca.

In the early 12th century Roger de Berecholles dwelt at Roger-stone Castle. It is recorded that he gave a gift of land to the Benedictine priory founded at Bassaleg. Rogerstone is a corruption of Roger's Town after de Berecholles, lord of the manor.

In 1776 an iron foundry was set up at Castle Works, a site beside the ruins of the castle. The whole of the site and plant was advertised in 1806 in the London newspaper, *The Star*: 'The lands for the most part are rich and fertile. The country is highly picturesque; remarkable for rich and diversified scenery, surrounding woods are remarkable for their beauty.'

The first industrial venture failed in 1879. Six years later Guest, Keen and Nettlefolds arrived. The site was cleared and extended, new mills and a nail factory were built. Guest, Keen and Nettlefolds remained until 1937 when their business was moved to East Moors, Cardiff.

Again the site was stripped and cleared in 1939 when the Northern Aluminium Company built a modern factory. Production began in late 1940. The De Havilland aircraft company built a small factory nearby and the wings of the Hurricane fighter planes were made from aluminium produced by the Northern Aluminium Company. Some 9,000 people were employed and many 'bussed in' from places as far apart as Brynmawr, Abertillery, Caerphilly and Llanbradach. The aluminium factory now employs only 800 people.

The Great Western Railway company employed many people at the shunting yards and freight area known as 'The Sidings'. Most freight was moved by rail and the Rogerstone depot served the lower parts of the Western and Sirhowy valleys. The nearest other depot was at Aberbeeg. Eventually the depot was phased out during reorganisation.

During the Second World War three German bombs were dropped on the village. In the spring of 1941 seven people were killed at High Cross. On 7th October 1941, eleven people were killed at Park Avenue, Tydu. The third bomb fell at Groes Farm but cattle were the only casualties. Because of the importance of the Northern Aluminium Company and De Havilland factories we suffered the indignity of a smoke screen. Hundreds of crude-oil burning stoves were placed along the main road through the village and were lit at nightfall. Thick, black, greasy and obnoxious fumes were emitted through the chimneys. No one would venture out after dark unless it was absolutely necessary.

Rogerstone holds a good record on education. In 1859 a cottage school was built at Tydu (Top Rogee) for the tinplate workers' children. The Rogerstone Henllys Board school opened in 1876. In fact there were three schools, one for boys, one for girls and an infants department. Today we have three good primary schools; one at Mount Pleasant estate, one at High Cross and the third at Cefn Wood estate. Senior pupils attend the excellent comprehensive school at Bassaleg.

A community centre shares the Cefn Wood complex. Adult education classes are held there. There is a very active bowls club with teams for men and women, the pitches for soccer and rugby are floodlit, and a badminton court is housed in the main hall. At the Welfare grounds at Tydu there is an excellent cricket field with an all weather wicket, two football pitches, tennis courts, a mini golf course and a children's play area.

Rogerstone has a silver band which has been in existence for over 40 years; they have won many prizes and cups in national and local contests. There is also a male voice choir – the Alcan Singers – which is pleasing to listen to. These singers give many performances for charitable organisations.

After the war we lost our beautiful green look. New houses were built on the High Cross fields and today there are hundreds of houses in this area. A private housing estate was built north of the canal at the Cefn, and a small estate of private houses was built at Court Gardens. A sheltered home complex – St John's Court – is very well cared for. The complex is on a flat site beside our few shops and the bus stops.

To provide for all these houses, etc, four farms were lost – Plain Farm, John's Farm, Vicarage Farm and Pontnewydd Farm (for a power station) – as well as the trees of two woods, Cefn Wood and Maes Wood. We also lost three market gardens, one of which was a lovely cherry orchard, and countless fields.

In 1776 the population of Rogerstone was 447 – in 1993 it

was approximately 12,000. Prior to 1974 we were part of Magor and St Mellons Rural District; at this time the boundaries were changed and we were absorbed into Newport Borough. We lost our village identity and became a mini industrial area for Newport with far too many factory units.

On 1st September 1991, almost 3,000 people gathered around the Tydu (Top Rogee) area to witness a happy event – the demolition of the Rogerstone power station. Built in 1954 it was obsolete almost as soon as it was completed. It produced electricity for 25 years and then went out of production. At eleven o'clock on that Sunday morning the cooling towers and the high stack were demolished by controlled explosions. The cheering of the multitude was almost as loud as the explosions.

Despite the industrialisation Rogerstone is a good place to live. The people are good, honest friendly folk. There is no vandalism and the police have little work to do.

Rogiet

The village of Rogiet, population approximately 1,000, is more commonly known to rail travellers as Severn Tunnel Junction. It incorporates two other villages, Ifton and Llanvihangel.

Rogiet is said to take its name from a manor house named Rogergalt, which was built by Roger de Gammage, one of William of Normandy's knights. The land on which the manor was built was given to him by William as a reward for his services during the invasion of Britain in 1066. The building still stands and is known as Manor Farm. The Domesday Book refers to Rogiet as 'Rodyat', meaning 'a gap in the hills'.

Adjacent to the Manor Farm is St Mary's Church, which was originally dedicated to St Hilary. The 12th century church has a square Norman tower with a 'thimble' on the top and is noted for the extra long chancel, which is longer than the nave. The well maintained lawn-type churchyard has won an award for being the best kept in Gwent within its class.

In 1903 the church was restored and enlarged to allow for the

Rogiet windmill

influx of railway workers into the area, due to the opening of the Severn Tunnel in 1886 and the marshalling yards nearby. A brass plaque was unveiled in the church in 1987 to mark the centenary of the opening of the Severn Tunnel; this year 1987 also saw the closing of the marshalling yards, due to railway reorganisation.

There is an ancient standing stone in a field near the village, known locally as the Devil's Quoit. Legend has it that the stone was hurled by the Devil from nearby Gray Hill and landed in the field. It is said that anyone trying to remove this stone would forfeit their life.

Rogiet windmill, the ruins of an old corn mill, stands on a high point looking across the river Severn. It is believed to date from the early 16th century, although the earliest recorded reference is in the 1851 census.

During the Second World War Rogiet WI members bought a canning machine. Members canned vegetables and fruit, thus ensuring a good supply for local needs. The machine was later donated to the Wolvesnewton Folk Museum, where it can still be seen.

Carnivals were very well supported by local people, with almost everyone being involved, young and old alike. One character who was extremely popular was Mr Alec Hayes. He was a great comic and musician. He composed a piece of music entitled *The sinking of the Titanic*. His death around 1960 was a sad loss to Rogiet.

The church and Methodist chapel work closely together. The Methodists held their first meetings in a reading room, until their new building was completed in 1933. Founder members have sons and daughters still active there today.

In 1942 an association was formed, to be known as the Rogiet Gardeners and Allotment Association, the purpose of which was to provide a service to gardeners, selling a variety of goods ranging from cement, tar and creosote, to seed potatoes and numerous garden aids. Membership fees were a shilling per year. Today the Association is still active and is run by retired railwaymen.

For many years a busy cattle market was held weekly in Rogiet and the Roggiet Hotel still has a room called the Market Room.

In 1920 an Operatic Society was formed and produced many excellent productions. After 20 years membership began to decline and the society decided to amalgamate with Caldicot Operatic. This proved successful and is very well appreciated, producing shows twice yearly.

Also in the village, Red Cross first aid classes were held for young people. Some of the youngsters are now Red Cross workers themselves. They serve teas and help raise funds for the Cheerful Club, which is run weekly by a dedicated committee and held in the community hall, adjacent to the primary and junior school. This latter has a very good reputation and it won the National Curriculum Award for 1992/1993.

St Arvans 🌿

Situated at the gateway of the picturesque Wye valley, St Arvans is a rural village with a population of approximately 550. From the early part of the 19th century the village folk were employed at the blacksmith's, the carpenter's shop, local farms and Squire Clay's estate.

Up to the late 1950s local people brought their horses to be shod by Mr Jones, the blacksmith, to the amusement and entertainment of the local children. Now the only reminder of the blacksmith is the name Forge Gardens, a small estate for retired residents.

One of the main characteristics of the village is the Fountain, a unique monument in this country, where the horses used to stop and drink during their journeys. Whilst little is known of its origin it is believed that an exact replica can be found in Durban, South Africa. It has been a meeting place for old and young for many generations.

Not far away stands the memorial hall built in memory of those who died in the First World War. It was opened in 1924, when it had a billiard room and a tennis court alongside; these amenities have now disappeared to make way for an extension and car park.

After the Second World War carnivals were held annually together with village sports days. A successful drama group was formed, playing to full houses, a Gilbert and Sullivan society entertained audiences for many years, and an annual pantomime was held. Sadly all are now disbanded. However, a village produce society has been meeting monthly for over 30 years, and every August stages a produce show. The WI also meets there, as do the Scouts, a playgroup is thriving and at the other end of the scale is the retirement society.

The one famous cricketer to hail from St Arvans was Mr Johnny Clay, who played for Glamorgan and England. The village cricket and football teams are still forces to be reckoned with, playing at the adjacent park where the first tourists to the lower Wye valley came to see Piercefield on the edge of St Arvans.

Piercefield was purchased in 1736 by Colonel Valentine Morris of St Vincent, who acquired his wealth in the Windward Isles. His son, also Valentine, brought his bride to Piercefield where they lived in princely style. About 1753 he began to lay out the grounds, with several named views: the Alcove, the Grotto, the Double View, the Great Beech Tree, the Top of the Hill, Lover's Leap, the Temple and the Wyndcliffe. He allowed tours twice a week; carriages had to be left at the gate and re-entered at St Arvans after the walk to see the views.

In 1924 the famous Chepstow racecourse was opened in Piercefield Park. This was where Sir Gordon Richards rode eleven consecutive winners. During the war it was taken over as a landing strip and maintenance depot for the forces. These included many nationalities and later on Italian prisoners of war. Valentine Morris's mansion was used for target practice, the ruins of which still remain today. The famous views still form part of the Wye Valley Walk.

The church and village of St Arvans take their name from the little-known St Arvan (Arfan). Tradition says he was a fisherman who died when his coracle overturned in the Wye. The church is an old foundation with a clear link of 1,000 years. It was extensively modified in the 19th century, but still retains part of the Norman chancel and priest's door. In AD 955 a deacon claimed sanctuary in the church after killing a farm worker. The family of the murdered man broke into the church and killed him before the altar. The violation of the sanctuary was looked upon as a worse scandal than the killings.

An old wedding custom was 'roping' the bride and groom as they left the church. The pair were not allowed to pass until money was handed over to the local children. The school is situated near the church. It was opened in 1873 with a teacher and 39 pupils. The headmaster kept a keen eye on the children's behaviour both inside and outside school hours. David Broome, of show jumping fame, is a former pupil. Unfortunately in 1988, as in many rural villages the school closed and children now catch a bus to Chepstow.

In close proximity to the village stood the Mare pool from where, on moonlight nights, a lady riding a white horse is reputed to emerge and ride across the fields. With road improvements the pool and ghost seem to have disappeared.

There is still a village store, a post office and one local inn; all other inns and the local chapel are now private dwellings. The residents, unlike their predecessors, now have to commute to nearby towns such as Cardiff and Bristol to work.

St Brides Wentloog 🦪

St Brides Wentloog is a small rural community lying to the west of Newport. It is bounded by the Bristol Channel to the south and the main Fishguard to Paddington railway line to the north.

The main occupation of its inhabitants is farming. The area is flat and fertile and drained by a series of reens or wide watercourses. It is protected from the rise and fall of the channel tides by a sea wall. At the turn of the century most of the area was owned by the Tredegar estate and farmed by tenants. In the 1950s the estate was sold, some of the farms being bought by tenants. As farms expanded and mechanised some of the farmhouses and farmworkers' cottages were no longer needed and as they became vacant were sold off, many to people working in the town.

At one time the village had a lighthouse, two public houses, two chapels, a shop, school, church and a village hall. Now only the two public houses and village hall are in regular use. The lighthouse, two chapels and school have been converted to houses and the church is closed, being in need of extensive renovation. The ex-servicemen's hall was built in the 1920s on land donated by Lord Tredegar with money raised by the people of the village. In 1992 the old wood and tin hall was demolished and replaced by a modern purpose-built building.

Before the motor car St Brides was a popular place for a day out for the people of Newport. They came in charabanc or by horse and cart and on foot to spend the day on the foreshore where there was a swimming pool filled by the tide and a cafe, among other things.

St Brides' most famous son is David Llewellyn Harding (Lyn), the Shakespearian actor, who was born at the Church House Inn in October 1867. He first appeared on a London stage in 1902. When the village school, which he attended, was closed a plaque hanging there in his memory was returned to the Church House Inn.

St Maughans and the Maypole 🦢

St Maughans and the Maypole straggle up the hill from Tregate Bridge on the Welsh side of the Monnow, to meet what used to be the main Rockfield to Grosmont road before the village was bypassed by the Newcastle toll road. The bridge must have been fairly important strategically at one time, being the first river crossing north of Monmouth, and there are two sturdy little manor houses on either side to keep an eye on it.

The village is full of 'used-to-be's'; there is a stone stump by the side of the road at the top which is said to have been the base of an old stone cross. Nearby there is a tangled patch of brambles that used to be a drill hall, where 'hops' drew would-be dancers on their bicycles from miles around. There is a cottage round the corner that used to be a pub called The Royal Onion. St Maughans' green was enclosed somewhere near Green Farm and lost to the village; there's even a bus stop.

In spite of this rather mournful evidence of a lively past, St Maughans is not a ghost village. Community life is based on the church, the Sunday newspaper rota and farmers borrowing things from one another. The church is situated about half a mile from the village on the old road. Principally it is a 13th century building with a pretty border lantern tower and two massive oak pillars. The church is probably visited as never before since appearing on the route plan of a prize-winning circular walk, cleared and signposted by the Gwent Countryside Warden and his volunteers. The walkers ramble in flocks and picnic in the churchyard but rarely come in to the services.

St Mellons 🦢

The village of St Mellons lies on the busy A48 Cardiff to Newport road. Well, old St Mellons does but the giant new St Mellons runs from the south side of that road nearly down to the foreshore of the Bristol Channel. Once coaches to London came through the village on the route from West Wales; they turned up the road between the two inns – The White Hart (with its mounting block still standing outside to this day) and The Blue Bell, into Tyr Winch Road, up the Druidstone Road, over Penylan down into Bassaleg and thence to Newport. This was part of a Roman road leading to Bassaleg.

That was, however, a bygone age – cities always extend their boundaries and landmarks disappear, like thatched cottages and the village smithy, but the ancient village church still stands above the village. The church is dedicated to St Melon, born so it is believed in Cardiff, who died in Rouen having been its bishop in AD 314. It is a large church dating from 1360 with a long nave, many original pews and two side chapels. It has one of the best examples of a plain cradle roof holding a rood loft. The church has a lively congregation who are active in raising funds for a new roof, and its services are well attended.

Near the church stood the village school. This old building had once been the village poorhouse but it was finally destroyed by fire started by vandals in 1989. The school had been the hub of the village, standing on the Ton where many years ago fairs were held to celebrate St Melon's day on 22nd October each year. Now the children go up St Mellons Hill to the new estate to school. But St Mellons has so many activities going on which thrive to this day. The church and the Baptist chapel in Tyr Winch Road; the WI founded over 70 years ago still meets every week in the village hall which accommodates young and old; Brownies; Cubs; a Senior Citizens club each Thursday; Whist Club; Venture Scouts; church socials plus a nursery school each morning – the list is endless. The hall facilities are so good that there is an excellent troupe of village entertainers who put on musicals, plays, and a pantomime each year which is as good as any put on by a professional theatre.

St Mellons has had its hours of glory. In 1921 the Prince of Wales, the uncrowned Edward VIII, opened an educational centre, met local ex-servicemen and visited the sports and social club. He was given a bouquet by five year old Thursa Shepstone who grew up to teach in the village school. The Queen came in 1971 to open Eastern Avenue into Cardiff. But perhaps St Mellons' most notorious character was the pirate Henry Morgan, born in Llanrumney Hall, now a public house surrounded by housing, who eventually was knighted and made governor of Jamaica in 1674.

Leafy lanes still exist in St Mellons and if one takes a walk along Began Road leading to Cefn Mably, once the mansion of the Kemeys family, one goes along the Began valley where the naturalist R. M. Lockley lived in the 1920s. Here he wrote books on the bird life, writing of corncrakes and nightingales which have long since gone and been replaced by lorries on the M4 rushing above the lane. R. M. Lockley moved to Skokholm in Dyfed and there started the first bird observatory in the world in 1927.

Every year St Mellons Show is held in the fields near Cefn Mably. It has gone on for over 120 years and every August people throng to this popular event. There are classes for everything – cattle, pigs, sheep, goats; horse-riding events; flowers and flower arranging; a dog show – you name it and it is there.

St Mellons may have changed but the old families still live here. The farms have been swallowed up by new housing estates in new St Mellons but the Jones family whose land and farms disappeared are still well in evidence in village life and Bridge Farm in Bridge Road is still a working farm, the last one in St Mellons itself. Old houses have changed their status. Ty-to Maen became the William Nichol Convalescent Home and now it is going to change again, its future undecided. Wern Fawr Farm was taken over by the Electricity Board whose huge luxurious offices front onto the A48, giving employment to many living in the area, most of whom however commute to Cardiff or Newport to earn their living today. Quarry Hill House, home of Sir William Cope, was turned into an old people's home but that was closed and its future is unknown.

Basically, however, all is still well here. Each July a village fête is held in the playing field and the WI makes Welsh cakes and provides teas. The church celebrates harvest with a Harvest Supper. The post office still functions, the village shop is still open all hours, and each November we remember the fallen of two World Wars and on the village cenotaph the wreaths are laid for the men of St Mellons who went to war and did not return.

Shirenewton & Mynyddbach

Over 2,000 years ago, in the Iron Age, the foundations of what is now Shirenewton were laid when the Silurians built a fort. Later the Romans actually built a road through the area which was to be the village and finally, between 1086 and 1129, the Sheriff's New Town was born. Originating in a clearing in the forest, Tre Newydd Gelli Fach, or New Town in the Little Grove was created and is ascribed to Walter Fitzroger, Sheriff of Gloucester and Constable of England. Fitzroger already owned the tenement of Caldicot and was responsible to Henry I for the administration of the west of England. The lordship of Caldicot and Newton remained together until the mid 19th century.

Standing peacefully on a hill overlooking the Caldicot Levels, Shirenewton gives the impression that the most radical changes it has experienced have been the coming of electricity, the telephone and automobiles and even these events did not trouble its tranquillity over much. A sleepy village, its appearance belies its wealth of history for those who care to plumb the depths of its rich past.

The church tower is 13th century and there is an elaborate south porch, containing a parvis or priest's room. The church was endowed with a rectory and 60 acres of land, not only for worship, but also for defence purposes. Messages could be signalled to Itton Court and then to the garrison in Chepstow. Dedicated to St Thomas a Becket, the church contains some fine stone carvings, one of which is of the patron saint and another of William Blethyn who was a figure of note, born in the village in the 16th century and later made bishop of Llandaff. The nave features a marble memorial to Captain Liddel VC of the Coldstream Guards, who was among the regiment's officers chosen to protect the Royal Family. It is interesting to

Church of St Thomas a Becket, Shirenewton

note that four incumbents in the 17th century were also bishops of Llandaff.

Not far from the church, among the trees, one can spy the roofs and chimneys of Shirenewton Hall, where Edward Lowe, the botanist, died in 1900. He wrote many books on the cultivation of woodland ferns and some species of these may be found around the churchyard walls. More recently, Shirenewton Hall made a claim to fame when it was used as the setting for the television drama *The Woman He Loved*. The stars Anthony Andrews and Jane Seymour caused quite a stir while filming was in progress and travellers became more than a little confused by the roadsigns being changed and postboxes etc being festooned with ivy to conceal them. However, it did not take long for peace to fall once more in this quaint backwater.

Other means of worship also went on in Shirenewton. The

Quakers or Society of Friends were known to have met in village homes from 1688, until their meeting house was built in 1734–5 for the princely sum of £204 18s 8d which included £26 for the purchase of the land. The meeting house is now a private dwelling, but the Friends' burial ground, dating from 1700 can still be seen on the road from Shirenewton to Mynyddbach.

Of course, some people worshipped the 'Demon Drink' and Shirenewton and its twin village of Mynyddbach have always provided more than their fair share of places in which to imbibe! The inns were obviously an important way of village life over the years and there were around seven or eight of them, four of which still exist; The Tredegar Arms, The Tan House, The Carpenters Arms and The Huntsman Hotel. The latter stands at the junction of what were two turnpike roads, Chepstow to Usk and Crick to Devauden Green. In the 1800s it was known as The Cross Hands and children used to run down from the villages to collect the post. One owner of this inn, Bill Benjamin was well known locally as a boxer.

Mynyddbach, once a small hamlet dotted with stone cottages, has now been modernised and added to but still retains its aura of old worldliness. Several of the houses bear signs of having been other than just homes. Pear Tree Cottage was once the home and workplace of the local cobbler and across the road, Mynyddbach House was the bakery. This house was also owned at one time by a Miss Thomas who became Lady De Havilland. Just prior to the First World War, people who were children at the time remember the lady and her husband landing in a plane, which must have been a biplane of the earlier type, on the 20 acre field above The Cross Hands, for a visit to her family. Another cottage down Weyloed Lane once housed a dame school. At least one villager remembers, as a child, her grandmother telling her that she had attended in the 1840s. The dame taught in one room, while her daughter took in washing in the scullery.

Unfortunately the twin villages have now become, in the main, dormitories for those working in Bristol and further afield. This, however, does not prevent them from being extremely attractive and from being able to offer lovely scenery, country walks and a very friendly atmosphere.

Skenfrith 🦋

Skenfrith is a small village in the north eastern corner of the county, twelve miles east of Abergavenny, 13 miles south of Hereford and about ten miles from Ross-on-Wye and Monmouth. People from both home and abroad visit here in considerable numbers because it is a very pretty village which in its essentials has changed little down the ages.

Skenfrith is also the name of a parish of 4,858 acres and was the centre of a medieval manor based upon the castle which was co-terminous with the parish.

St Bridget is the patroness of the church. She came from Kildare in Ireland where she was abbess of a monastery for both men and women and about whom many fine apocryphal tales are told; not least that one afternoon she converted Skenfrith to Christianity and established a church there and after tea the same day, went on to Bridstow outside Ross, where she did the same thing, to the great benefit of the community.

There has always been a puzzle about the name Skenfrith and there are two main explanations of its origin. That put forward by Mr Joseph Bradney in his *Hundreth of Skenfrith* is that the name was originally Ynys Cynfraeth and Cynfraeth was the 6th century son of Cyndrwyn, Prince of part of Powys. The second explanation favoured by Professor Bowen of Aberystwyth, is that it derived from Bridget and the church. The one is a civil and the other is an ecclesiastical explanation.

Joseph Bradney also adds that at the time of the Conquests, Skenfrith belonged to Bach, the eighth son of Gwaethfoed, Prince of Cardigan and that at the time, the castle was probably a small earth and timber fort.

The Normans conquered this area during the lifetime of William Fitz Osbern, Earl of Hereford and his son Roger is referred to as Lord of Gwent. It was about this time that the Normans built their first castle which consisted of a rectangular enclosure roughly 700 by 400 feet, with a motte at its south west corner. This rectangle included most of the ground on which the present village stands and included the church and churchyard although the present structure had not then been built.

This earth and timber castle stood until after 1200 when it was rebuilt in stone by Hubert de Burgh. It was built in one piece by Hubert and there are no observable additions. It does not seem to have been in much use after 1300. It is an irregular four-sided structure with corner towers and a central keep. It was surrounded on three sides by a 40 foot wide moat which has since been filled in. A brief account of its history is placarded in the castle and a comment on the castle by a recent American visitor is worth recording, 'Gee, ain't it grand to have a castle in your backyard'.

The church of St Bridget close to the castle was also originally built by Hubert de Burgh and the present tower, nave and chancel are Hubert's work. Both the north and south aisles have been altered and extended laterally in later years. In its early years it was probably unique as a parish church because of its style and proportions.

It contains within it many features of great interest, not least a 15th century cope, a 16th century decorated tomb and box-pew of the Morgan family, an original stone altar and font with staples for locking it against holy water thieves, a panel of the old rood screen in the priest's desk, an Elizabethan parish map with south at the top and north at the bottom and a whole history of the church seating from Tudor times to present day. Further details of this fine Early English church with its dovecote can be found in the church. It was reroofed by the Rev Macadam and villagers in the 1970s.

The mill on the south side of the castle is on the site of a medieval mill which was still in good repair in 1611. The present mill was substantially repaired in 1867 and is still in working order with Mr Malcolm Edwards as miller. His father and grandfather were millers in Skenfrith before him.

There may not have been a mill here when the castle was occupied because it would have weakened the water defences of the castle.

Skenfrith church has a peal of six bells and it is just possible that the first bells were cast more or less on site. This often happened because of the availability of wood on the site needed to cast the bells. The Bell Inn near the Monnow Bridge may have been named in memory of this event.

The judge Sir Richard Morgan, who condemned Lady Jane Grey to death, lived here at Blackbrook. In his will he left 6s 8d for repairs to Skenfrith church.

Once a bustling community, it was on the drove road from Wales to the English towns, with a toll gate which in 1611 yielded the king a rent of 13s 4d a year. There were four commons used by tenant farmers for 'herbage and pannage' on annual payment of yet again 13s 4d to the king. On the death of a tenant, a heriot (tax) of his second best beast was due to the king.

There were at one time four churches here – St Bridget's, the Baptist chapel (both still in use), the Wesleyan chapel (now a house) and the Catholic church, built in 1843 on a site earlier given by Hubert de Burgh to the Cistercian monks of Abbey Dore and later demolished (only the graveyard and yew trees remaining).

In 1895 there was a shoemaker, grocer, draper, blacksmith, miller, three pubs and a post office. Now only the church, castle, mill, houses, inn and motel form the central attraction along the river, with most of the community spread along small roads around and on the hillsides.

There was schooling for Skenfrith children from about 1832. The village school, at Norton, which closed in 1991 with twelve children on the register, was built in 1877 as a Board school for 120 children, at a cost of £1,200. Average attendance then was 80, with highest attendance after the First World War. During the depression of the 1880s the headmaster's salary was cut to £40 – at one time it had been as much as £90. Children paid from a penny to threepence a week, depending on age. Entries from the headmaster's diary (1876–1903) include –

9.8.1877 Chastised William Walker for foul and disgusting language uttered in the playground to Mrs Fornachon. (Put him across the knee.)

13.6.1895 40% absence, cause is great temperance demon-
stration at Pontrilas.

9.7.1900 Men scarce (war), boys gone to thin roots, cut
thistles and frighten crows.

3.7.1903 Several gone to Abergavenny to see show (Buffalo
Bill).

Talywaun 🌿

Talywaun ('Tal' means the flat land, 'Waun' means the moor) lies
along a spur of land below the mountains on the western side
of the Afon Lwyd valley. Two hundred years ago, it must have
been a tranquil place, with only a few stone-built farmhouses and
cottages built to withstand all weathers, their inhabitants making
their living from the land.

It was the exploitation of iron which first brought people to the
area in search of work, the three main iron-works being at Varteg,
Golynos and the British. Local mines provided the raw materials
and with the discovery of coal, industry flourished and rows of
houses were hastily built to accommodate the workers. Coal was
taken out of the ground by means of 'levels' being worked into the
coal outcrops all along the western hillsides. Sometimes different
minerals were found, but anything of use was brought out.

'At three or four o'clock every day, the streets were filled with a
black stream of men on their way home,' remembers one resident,
while another recalls her husband coming home from the Graig
Ddu clay mine. 'He was an ostler, looking after the horses which
pulled the trucks full of clay. He came home just as dirty as any
collier and there were no pit baths then. He had to bathe in a tin
bath in front of the fire as we did not have a bathroom where we
lived then. The clay was used at the brick works on Pentwyn.'

The most notable landmark in Talywaun is the viaduct, which
was built in 1876 under the direction of John Gardner to carry
the LNWR railway line from Talywaun to Blaenafon and thence
to Brynmawr. In 1912, the line was opened to passenger traffic
and became linked to the GWR line running down to Pontypool.

There was a station at Talywaun, just off Church Road, where one could catch a train either up or down, and many people travelled to work this way. On the land behind the church were many sidings and at Talywaun Cross there was a level crossing, with a signal box opposite The Globe pub, where lines branched towards Varteg and other collieries.

One of these was Llanerch colliery, a mile or so away round the mountain. It was a deep pit with several slopes at different depths. On 6th February 1890, a disaster occurred, killing 176 men and boys and devastating many families in the area. Graves and memorial tablets can be seen at local chapels and churches.

A church was built here in 1832, first as a chapel in the parish of Trevethin but becoming the parish church of Abersychan in 1844. It is constructed of grey stone and is plain in design, being said to have been built by the British Iron Company along the lines of a workshop. Its first vicar was the Rev Bluett, but it became known as St Thomas's church after a later incumbent, Rev William Rees Thomas, who became very well regarded for his excellent sermons. Services were at first conducted in English and Welsh alternately, as they also were at Pisgah chapel. Started in 1827, this building is of red brick and has a large school room beside it. Other chapels are Noddfa on Church Road and Zion Pentecostal which now occupies the premises formerly The Albert.

There used to be many small houses and shops and pubs: The Black Horse, The Nag's Head, The Globe, The Albert, The Greyhound, The Britannia, The Vulcan, The Golynos, The White Horse, The Railway, The Constitutional and The Commercial being some. Some of these have long gone as have many shops, but there remain The Albert Stores and a hairdresser's salon near The Globe; a newsagent's, greengrocer's and fish and chip shop opposite the church; and the post office with general store on Wellington Road.

A school was built early in the 19th century and was known as the British, catering at first for the children of the iron-workers. In time, there were separate infants and elementary schools on the same site on Church Road, eventually becoming a secondary modern school. The stone buildings and the two school houses can still be seen, but are in a derelict state except for the section which has housed the Mayflower Christian school for some years.

No railway lines remain, passenger services ceasing in 1941 and the last coal train coming down at the closure of Big Pit at Blaenafon in 1981. The Talywaun station buildings house transport and other businesses and the track has been widened and roughly surfaced to form a leisure route for walkers, cyclists and horse riders – a three mile track, quietly meandering away southwards to Pontnewynydd without the noise of traffic. To the north, the line has not been developed, other than by the erection of safety barriers on the viaduct. Walkers can enjoy a beautifully peaceful ramble all the way to Blaenafon, but the surface is suitable for bicycles only as far as Shop Road, just beyond the site of Varteg station.

Other exhilarating walks begin at Talywaun, leading over moors and mountains to give splendid views towards the Severn. Relics of industrial history abound but the scars of mineral extraction are fast disappearing as nature's green mantle reclothes the remaining tips and opencast sites. The rugby club occupies old sidings, while a large area of young trees is thriving above the Bucks Level where until recently a garden centre and golf driving range operated.

One eyesore remains, a dangerous expanse of land between Talywaun and the British, land which has been so subjected to disturbance that its original form is quite lost. Undermined by old coal levels, its natural drainage intercepted and diverted in the industrial era, it was infilled and levelled in the 1970s, leaving a scene of dereliction overlooked by the oldest of cottages and the newest of houses. Many plans have been made for its reclamation, many hopes raised and dashed. It is probable that the next few years will see Talywaun yet again under a coat of coal dust because open cast mining has been selected as the preferred means of financing the restoration of this area – the wheel has come full circle.

Tintern 🦌

'We stopped to examine the rich architecture of the west front: but the door being opened the inside perspective of the church called forth an instantaneous burst of admiration and filled me with delight, such as I scarcely ever experienced on a similar occasion.' (William Coxe, *An Historical Tour Through Monmouthshire*, London 1801.)

By the time William Coxe visited Tintern Abbey it had already become an internationally famous tourist attraction. It has often been referred to as the most beautiful ruin in Britain, although it has lost some of its romantic character since the ivy was removed from its walls. The beautiful watercolour by Turner proves this point.

The abbey of Tintern was founded in 1131 by Walter de Clare for monks of the Cistercian order. St Bernard is the great saint of the order. There were strict rules of silence and a simple diet and much emphasis on austerity. The 'white monks' as they were called wore habits of white undyed wool.

The new community grew rapidly as more land was bestowed on the abbey and more monks were recruited locally. The dissolution of the monasteries 400 years later, during the 16th century brought an abrupt end to the lifestyle of the monks. The treasures and roofing were stripped and stone removed for buildings elsewhere.

In 1990 Tintern celebrated the 900th anniversary of the birth of St Bernard. It was a lovely sunny Sunday morning and there was a happy atmosphere of song and prayer within the ancient ruins – a large congregation of people, with children seated on the grass, and clapping to the accompaniment of cymbals.

The interior of Tintern Abbey is even more beautiful than the exterior. Every arch and stone breathes a sublime antiquity and a strange tranquillity which make it easy to feel the presence of the white friars of so long ago. It is roofed only by the walls of Heaven and carpeted only with the grass of Earth and to be there is a spiritual experience.

Visitors to Tintern might wish to visit the old station in search of refreshment. In September 1975 it was opened to the public as a visitor centre and picnic site, based on the Wye Valley Railway. It is a site well worth a visit. Built originally in the Victorian era to revitalise the industrial and commercial life of the Lower Wye Valley and to provide a passenger service, the site probably attracts more visitors today than it ever did as a railway. The signal box is now an exhibition area for local arts and crafts.

A few years ago there was a delightful exhibition about the life and written work of Flora Klickmann, 'the lady of the flower patch'. For over 20 years in the early part of this century, she wrote about the life of her small cottage near Tintern. She was passionately concerned about the gradual destruction of the countryside long before environmentalism and ecology became fashionable.

The picturesque appearance of the ruins is considerably enhanced by their position in a valley watered by the meandering Wye and backed by woodlands which often rise from the river, uniting a delightful mixture of wildness and culture.

Tredunnock 🐿

Situated just over a mile from Llantrissent, the two villages share a vicar, a Women's Institute and buses. In the middle of Tredunnock is a green complete with a well sunk in 1870. Nearby is a farm with a large chestnut tree, which produces much sought after chestnuts. There is a row of what were once council houses now mostly privately owned, a large vicarage, a church, church hall and public house.

Considerable competition occurs over the Best Kept Village in Gwent. Tredunnock has won several times and once came second as the Best Kept Village in Wales. The gardens are a joy to everyone including those who toil.

There are about 150 people living in and around this village, with about 14 children and a considerable number of retired or pensioned people. The village suffers more traffic than Llantrissent, with a half mile walk to an hourly bus service between Newport and Usk. The village, being high, is not flooded by the river and unlike Llantrissent, has the benefit of mains water.

The church is approached by a gate erected in memory of those who died in the First World War. In the churchyard is an area of reburied graves from Kemeys, a churchyard which was swallowed up by the A449. There is a tomb dedicated to Eleanor Isabella, only child of Sir John Franklin, explorer of the North West Passage. The unfortunate daughter was visiting the area and cared for a child with a 'deadly malady' in 1860. The child recovered but poor Eleanor died. Inside the partly Norman church is a well preserved Roman tombstone to a soldier, Julius Julianus, found nearby.

The bridge crossing the river Usk was built in 1820, replacing an old wooden structure. The house opposite the present Newbridge Inn was once a tavern known as The Fisherman's Rest. Many houses on the land winding above the river, have an enviable view across the Usk valley. Villagers enjoy their proximity to the waterway with such activities as walking, bird watching, fishing and other rural pastimes. The partially tidal character of the river is currently under threat by the proposal to build a barrage across the river at Newport.

Trellech 🦚

Trellech is one of the most beautiful and interesting villages in Gwent – indeed some would say the whole of Wales.

It is situated in a saucer-like depression at the top of a hill five miles south of Monmouth, on the Monmouth to Chepstow ridge road. At about 800 feet above sea level, it has an invigorating climate. Old inhabitants always used to say, 'Trellech is two coats colder than Monmouth', and in severe winters it is one of the first places to be cut off from the surrounding towns and villages by snow drifts.

Overlooking the village is the Beacon Hill, 1,000 feet above sea level, covered with conifers and managed by the Forestry

Commission. In the early 1950s a fire-watchers' tower was built on the summit and it was said that seven counties could be seen from the top of it. The tower is no longer there, but there is a car park and picnic place hidden among the trees from where can be seen the village of Trellech and wonderful views of the Welsh mountains in the distance.

There has been a great deal of controversy over the name 'Trellech'. It is generally agreed that the name means either the town of the stones or the three stones, though even experts in the Welsh language have differed over the years as to the exact meaning.

In historical documents written during the years 1223 to 1677 it has been spelt in at least 20 different ways from Trilec to Trellech (1677). Even today as you enter the village you will see on the signposts Trellech, Trelech or Trelleck, depending on which road you are travelling!

In 1894 the Revd Thomas Davies MA became vicar of Trellech. He was a Welsh-speaking Welshman with a deep resonant voice that filled the church. Several years later Miss Louise Gilbert of Penarth was appointed headmistress of the village school. She married a local man and became Mrs Franklin. From that time until the 1940s when Mrs Franklin died, the children of the school – two generations of some local families – were taught to spell the name of the village 'Trellech'.

Mrs Franklin ruled over her pupils with a rod of iron – or to be more accurate, with a very pliable cane. There are still some men in the area who can testify as to the strength of her arm! When a girl had to be corrected, the offender's sleeve was solemnly rolled up above the elbow and her forearm slapped soundly.

For a number of years in the 1920s and 1930s, Trellech school was closed for the summer holidays in July, not August as were the schools in the surrounding villages. This was because some families wanted to take their children to the local wimberry commons to pick the fruit, which was then taken to the market or shops in Monmouth. This provided a welcome addition to many family incomes.

Trellech school has a long and interesting history. The Rev

Zachary Babington, who was vicar of Trellech from 1670 to 1705, established a school charity and a lectureship charity with the vicar and four laymen as trustees. The first school was held in the cottage adjoining the church lychgate. In 1880 a new school, including a school house, was built on the Clock House Lands opposite the church. This building was used as the village school until 1987 when a large new primary school was built in the field at the back of the old school. Schools in the surrounding villages were closed and children from five to eleven years of age are now brought in by bus to the new Trellech county primary school.

After much legal argument, what used to be known as the Trellech church-endowed school has been returned to the parish of Trellech and is now called the Babington Centre. Trustees have been appointed and fundraising has begun in order to bring the building back into good repair for use as an educational and community centre.

As you approach Trellech, the first sign of the village is the tall, slender spire of St Nicholas's church. From the Chepstow road it is visible from three miles away. For a small village the church appears to be unusually large, but it must be remembered that in the Middle Ages Trellech Town was one of the most important towns in South Wales, holding borough status with its own mayor, charter and town seal. No charter has survived but several years ago the children of the village school, after much research, discovered the town seal and were allowed to make a copy of it.

Gradually, over a long period of time and after suffering from the Great Plague and a number of local wars, including the savagery of Owain Glyndwr, the town became the small and peaceful village that it is today.

Set in the centre of a large churchyard, beautifully maintained by a local gentleman who is spending his retirement dedicated to the upkeep of our local public places, St Nicholas's church is a splendid place to spend a peaceful hour or so. On a table near the south door there is usually a pile of leaflets giving a short history of the church, which is well over 600 years old. One of the most interesting things in the church is an ancient sundial, dating from 1689, showing carved representations of the three historic monuments of Trellech.

The first of these is locally known as Tump Terrett, situated behind the church and generally believed to be the remains of a very early motte and bailey castle. In the past it has always been considered to be very unlucky to dig there or make any kind of excavation!

The second site shows the Three Stones, known at that time as Harold's Stones and believed to be the site of a battle where King Harold was the victor. These days it is generally accepted that they are prehistoric. An old village story, handed down through generations, says that they were thrown there by Jack o'Kent and the Devil in a contest of strength, and if you look closely at the Skirrid mountain near Abergavenny you will see the hole in the side where Jacky Kent's heel pressed into the mountainside as he threw one of his stones.

The third side of the sundial shows the Virtuous Well, at one time known as St Anne's Well and famous for its healing powers.

At the lower end of the village is the Methodist chapel which was built in the 19th century. Church services are held on Sunday mornings and the chapel services on Sunday evenings. There is good co-operation between the two places of worship and members of each congregation are always ready to help with the fundraising efforts of the other. Both church and chapel are licensed to perform marriages but the chapel has no burial ground.

It used to be the custom to 'rope' the bride and groom after the wedding ceremony. As the happy couple drove slowly along the church path to the road, boys and girls held a rope across their path to impede their progress and refused to move until the bridegroom threw out a handful of coins as a ransom. In those days most bridegrooms were prepared beforehand with a pocketful of pennies, threepenny bits and sixpences.

Before the Second World War, Trellech was a farming community consisting of farmers, smallholders and tradesmen connected with the life of such a community. One family firm had a sawmill, made coffins, and performed the duties of undertakers. They were also carpenters, wheelwrights and blacksmiths, and there was another blacksmith's forge at the bottom end of the village.

A shop in the centre of the village sold a wide variety of goods and there was also a post office complete with a small local telephone exchange. Two pubs, the Lion Inn and the Crown Hotel (now known as the Village Green Restaurant) completed the amenities. These are all still in existence. The local hostelries have become well known for their food as well as for their drinks, and the telephone exchange has become automatic and covers a much wider area.

After the war a new housing estate catering for families and pensioners was built at the northern end of the village and new houses and bungalows have sprung up in various places. The old village pound, in which animals were impounded, has become a holiday cottage. There has been no village policeman for some years but the old court house has become a residence and still bears that name.

Although the area has remained largely agricultural, there are far fewer people living in the village who are connected with farming. Some of the newcomers are commuters who work in neighbouring towns – Bristol, Newport, Cardiff and even London.

For those who like to spend their leisure time in the company of other people there are a number of societies and organisations. The Village Produce Association meets monthly in the church hall and arranges various outings to gardens and places of interest. They also have an annual show in September. The WI and the Mothers' Union meet monthly and there is a local Crafts Society and a silver band with members drawn from the surrounding area. Several ecumenical youth clubs are organised by both church and chapel members.

The Trellech Society, 'for all those interested in ancient places, their environment, their history, their rural life and the preservation of the ancient features of Trellech', holds regular meetings and arranges an annual three day festival of music and flowers.

Trellech Grange ✎

Trellech Grange is situated between the two roads which run from Monmouth to Chepstow: one through the Wye Valley and the other through Trellech, Llanishen and Devauden.

Although it is still a mainly agricultural parish, there have been many changes over the years. In the 1841 census the occupations of the inhabitants were farmer, farm worker, miller, blacksmith, wood cutter, shepherd, saddler, wood dealer, wire cleaver, tin worker and forge man. The last three would probably have been employed at the forge at Pontysaison, which is in the Agiddy Valley at the lower end of the parish. Of those employed today, only the farmers work here; the remainder (which include teachers, computer specialists and insurance personnel) commute.

The local council has replaced the Court Leet, which used to meet at the Ship Inn. The Ship Inn and the Globe Inn are now private houses, and The Vine Tree has completely disappeared. Only the Fountain Inn remains.

Many centuries ago the land was owned and farmed by the abbot and monks of Tintern Abbey. Subsequently it passed to the Duke of Beaufort and afterwards the farms and most of the cottages were purchased by the Crompton Roberts family, who lived at Drybridge House in Monmouth. In that era there were gamekeepers, woodwards, masons and carpenters. These occupations have all gone, like those who worked at the forge. Today most of the properties are owner-occupied.

An 18th century map shows Trellech Grange on the main coach road from Bristol to Chester: the Severn being crossed at the Old Passage, thence to Chepstow, St Arvans, Trellech Grange, Trellech, the Gockett, Lydart and Monmouth before leaving the county.

The church is a small building which was originally a chapel of ease belonging to Tintern Abbey. The old registers refer to it as a chapel, which explains why the adjoining farm is called the Chapel Farm. The church registers for burials commence in the 1830s, but baptisms and marriages took place much earlier. The census of 1861 shows that a curate lived at Chapel Farm.

The two world wars brought many changes. The end of the first brought about the sale of the Crompton Roberts interest, when the farms were all for sale and the estate maintenance staff were no longer required. The end of the second caused another change, as with less labour needed on the farms, the cottages were sold and were bought either for retirement or for commuters to town businesses.

Undy & Magor ✑

The villages of Magor and Undy are situated between Newport and Chepstow, close to the bank of the river Severn and skirted by the M4 motorway.

Undy dates from the Roman invasion of our shores in AD 43. It is reputed that St Dubritius founded Undy's church in the 6th century for St Gwyndaf and his wife Wyndaf. Their names are believed to be the origin of the name Undy.

The village itself was destroyed during the Great Flood of 1606, and probably the only building of note remaining was the 12th century church, which had been built on a solid shelf of rock. Its bell, dated 1360, still summons the faithful to worship today. An Elizabethan chalice inscribed 1577 is still in use.

The church, now dedicated to St Mary, was originally governed by the monks of Goldcliffe Priory, who preached there regularly. For many years there was no rectory at Undy, but in the early 1700s Queen Anne presented a sum of money for the purchase of one.

The old church school is now the church hall, and during recent excavations the skeletons of two Roman soldiers were found, one with a spear protruding from his chest. They were both given a christian burial.

Undy has had its share of colourful characters. The village pigkiller was Mr Andrews, who was feared by local children. If they were cheeky to him he chased them. An unnamed minister of religion lived in a cottage which was known as 'Tea Pot Shed'. He was a heavy drinker, and kept his whisky in a teapot, and drank it from a tea-cup, presumably to fool his parishioners.

A Mr John Adams was always known as 'Johnny Oily', so called because he travelled the local villages in his van, selling everything from shoe laces to paraffin oil. He also sold chocolate and sweets which tasted of paraffin, but no one seemed to mind. He ran a shop called 'The Bon Bon' situated at the bottom of Vinegar Hill. This was so named as there was once a vineyard on the hill owned by Sir Roger St Maur, the first lord of the manor at Undy.

Other intriguing names include Dancing Hill where, old legend has it, fairies are to be seen dancing on midsummer eve. Lime Kiln Lane was the obvious name, as there were quite a number of lime stone quarries. Cottages built for the quarry workers are still standing and lived in today, known as Laurel Crescent.

During the winter months most of the moorland from Newport to Undy Bridewell was frozen solid, and skaters would skate the eight or so miles from Newport. Then a coach would take them home.

One of the highlights of the village was the annual fair. This was the Poultry and Flower Show. It was always well attended and created keen competition amongst the local gardeners.

Magor church was originally called St Leonard's in the 13th century and was known as the 'Cathedral of the Moors'. Every 6th November the village held a fair and this is depicted in the Roman calendar as St Leonard's Day.

After restoration of the church in 1866 it was rededicated St Mary's, the vicar at that time for some unknown reason changing the patron saint. St Mary's has six bells and you can still see the campanologists ringing to this day. St Mary's has an overhead room reached by a staircase from the inside of the church, said to have been used for a library and a schoolroom. A secret passage is still in existence and leads from the church to Manor Farm.

The Ebenezer Baptist chapel was built in 1816 and rebuilt in 1993. A short distance away from the chapel is Morgan's garage. This was built in the 12th century, and was originally a sawmill and later an undertaker's combined, with carpenters working at the rear making coffins. Behind the mill was a quay to moor boats.

The village had a thriving railway station which is now sadly closed. Local people have fought unsuccessfully to have it reopened.

Magor boasts a fine old village square, which contains a stone cenotaph to commemorate the dead of the two world wars. The cenotaph was set up in 1924 by the first Lady Rhondda.

Prior to the Second World War an old sea captain named Skipper Hale owned the Wheatsheaf Inn. He always kept his parrot in the bar to warn him if anyone entered. The parrot was very partial to beer and was often found drunk in the bottom of his cage after closing time.

Today, Undy and Magor are one community and expanding rapidly. Large housing estates are now built on the Cowleaze, Dinch Hill and Mill Common. Many of the residents commute to workplaces as far afield as Cardiff, Bristol and London, via the M4. A new service station opened two years ago at the Magor intersection. Some local people are employed at the relatively new Whitbread's brewery situated close by. Sadly a great change from what was predominantly an agricultural area.

The Frost Fair is now held in December and is probably a revival of the St Leonard's Fair from the 13th century. On May Day an annual fete is held in the square with many organisations participating, drawing both communities together.

Usk 🌿

Usk is a small town that has a village atmosphere. It is in the centre of Gwent and approached by good roads from all directions.

Usk has a history dating back beyond medieval times. It boasts a castle and priory, both now in ruins and privately owned, and a priory church built in Norman times. The church, St Mary's has seen various alterations over the centuries. Earlier, Usk was the site of the Roman settlement of Burrium. Indeed it is reputed to be the longest continuously inhabited settlement in Wales.

Running along the western boundary is the river Usk, popular with fishermen for its salmon and trout fishing. The river is also popular for people walking its banks, and for artists, capturing the beauty of the changing seasons in paint or pencil, the wooded hillsides provide an ever changing, colourful backcloth.

The inhabitants of Usk support a wide selection of organisations from Guides and Scouts for the younger age group to the Women's Institute and various church organisations for the adults. There are three thriving churches in the town; the parish church of St Mary, the Baptist church and the Roman Catholic church of St Francis Xavier and St David Lewis. Each church has its own interesting history.

St Mary's priory church was originally cruciform; its core is the early Norman tower. The priory was founded a little later – around 1135 – and housed a community of five Benedictine nuns,

Twyn square, Usk

one of only four nunneries in Wales. After the dissolution of the monasteries in 1535, the priory was granted to Roger Williams of Llangybi. The gravestone of the last prioress of Usk can be seen from the main path through the churchyard.

Another interesting tombstone is that of St David Lewis. David Lewis was ordained a Catholic priest in 1642. He was wrongly implicated in the Popish plot of 1678 and arrested in November of that year. He was imprisoned in Monmouth for a while before being returned to Usk to the prison in Bridge Street. On 27th August 1679 he was hanged and disembowelled on a site opposite to where the Roman Catholic church of St Francis Xavier and St David Lewis now stands. The church was built in 1847. On the last Sunday in August there is a pilgrimage organised from the church to the tomb of St David Lewis.

Of the three nonconformist chapels, the Baptist church built in 1842 is the only one remaining in use as a place of worship. The Wesleyan chapel and the Congregational church – or the United Reformed church as it became – were sold and have been converted into flats. However, the exteriors of these buildings remain unchanged.

In 1842 the new prison was built in Maryport Street. This replaced the former House of Correction in Bridge Street. The prison housed 80 male prisoners and 40 female. Over the years it has been a detention centre, a youth custody centre and a young offenders' institution. Following the prison riots in a number of prisons in 1990, Usk prison took on the role of Vulnerable Prisoner Unit.

Next to the prison is the Sessions House built in 1874. The Court of Quarter Sessions met there until the end of the Second World War. This court house is a fine example of Victorian architecture and has been the location for various films. It is now the local magistrates' court.

The thread of history runs through Usk in many ways, its buildings, its people and various deeds. Part of the county's history can also be seen in the Old Malt Barn which houses the Gwent Rural Life Museum.

The town crier! The very name conjures up a picture of a portly personage, resplendent in a scarlet robe and black tricorn hat, proceeding through the streets with measured tread and pausing at intervals to ring his bell and resonantly intone 'o yez, o yez', proclaiming solemn decrees of importance to the populace. Well, the town crier of Usk, as one resident remembers him, was quite different.

Billo Wisham was a small wizened, shabby, down at heel figure of a man who wore an over-long, once black overcoat. Either he had shrunk, or its original owner had been of well built stature. On his head he wore an old tweed check cap and around his precious throat a somewhat grubby muffler. Thus attired, Billo shuffled through every street in the town. Each time he stopped to clang his bell, little children stopped their play, dogs barked and housewives hurried to open their doors to listen to Billo's pronouncements. They had to listen hard too, for poor Billo suffered a speech impediment and his proclamation could easily be misinterpreted.

He started off with 'Take notice', then another clang of the bell, and maybe, 'A Grand Concert will be held in the town hall at seven o'clock, please all to attend. God save the King.' Or maybe it was 'A jumble sale, please all to attend, God save the King.' Or 'The town water will be turned off at two o'clock this afternoon, God save the King.' Bazaars, town carnivals and fancy dress parties, all had the same publicity and, loyal subject that Billo was, he always concluded with the prayer that the King might be saved.

Present day Usk has claimed its place through the Wales in Bloom competitions. Since first entering the competition in 1980 Usk has always been placed with the winners, coming first in its class nearly every year. Twice Usk has won the Britain in Bloom competition. These results reflect the hard and dedicated work put in by the Usk in Bloom Committee. The many floral displays in the town, the hanging baskets, window boxes and special display boxes attract visitors to the town, especially in July and August. Flowers, namely daffodils, are also an attraction in the spring. Daffodils are planted on the roadside verges of all the approaches to our town.

Whatever the season visitors are always welcome and appropriate refreshment is available to all, in the various inns, restaurants and coffee shops, before they go on their way.

Whitebrook 🌿

Whitebrook is one of the most attractive villages in Gwent. Like Tintern it shows little of its industrial past to the casual visitor, but a closer look reveals the existence of the old paper mills cleverly transformed into several residential properties, greatly enhanced by the remaining mill ponds.

The mills, of course, were run by water – a chain of ponds, some of the water from underground. It was a thriving industry providing useful local employment for villagers. It was fed by esparto grass imported all the way from Africa and brought over from Bristol by *Llandogo Trow* and sloop. The supplementary feed was our own local alderwood. Sadly, this employment died out about 1900 and only a couple of ivy-covered chimneys remain today.

What a pity there are no drawings or pictures to remind us of the industrial heyday of Whitebrook. There are the remains of a warehouse and yards on the banks of the Wye near its junction with the White Brook, which further illustrates the importance of the river as a means of transport in the former days. There is also a note about a paper mills outing dated 1880:

'The workers and their families embarked early in the
morning in a trow (barge) which drifted down the Wye on
the falling tide, to Chepstow, then sailed across the Severn
to Bristol via the Avon, their destination was the "Llandoger
Trow" and the zoo. The return journey made use of reverse
currents, the rising tide carrying the Trow smoothly upstream
from Chepstow via Tintern and Llandogo to Whitebrook.'

What a blissful outing. The return journey could not have taken less than 12 hours.

The village lies literally on the road between Llandogo and Penallt, a single narrow street winding its way up a wooded valley, alongside the tumbling White Brook with its succession of broad mill ponds which now grace some of the larger properties dotted along either side of the road.

Wolvesnewton

Wolvesnewton is a parish on the old Chepstow road five miles south east of Usk and eight miles north west of Chepstow.

The church of St Thomas à Becket is an old stone building, partly in the Early English style. It consists of a chancel, a nave, a south porch and a saddleback western tower that has three bells. It seats 200 people but the population today is just under 100. The register that dates from 1680 is very mutilated. The living is a rectory, annexed to Kilgwrwg in 1884. In 1891 there was a Congregational chapel near Devauden.

It is said that there were five court or manor houses: the farmhouse known as Cwrt-y-Gaer occupies the site of an ancient camp or stronghold; a large portion of the moat still remains. In the 19th century the lord of the manor was the Duke of Beaufort and the principal landowners were Colonel Rumsey and Walter Smedley. The parish was included in the United School Board District of East and West Newchurch, formed in 1874. The children used to attend the school of Devauden but this has since been closed and sold as a private dwelling.

Wolvesnewton today is a much-changed parish; farmland has been sold to neighbouring farms with the dwellings and out-buildings converted to other uses. A prime example has been the Folk Museum at the Model Farm, which was previously Hill Farm. The museum opened in the late 1970s and put Wolvesnewton very much on the map with the arrival of many visitors from far and wide to the area. The unique 'cross' style of the buildings adds to the attraction. Also much use has been made of the restaurant as a most welcome venue for social functions in the area since the loss of the church hall to the rectory as an additional outbuilding to that property. At the end of 1993, however, the house was sold off and it is now renamed Beaufort House. The museum has closed whilst the owners wait for a decision from the Welsh Office on a new site in a different area.

Two other farms, Clydach and Cwrt-y-Gaer have also been split up, the latter into three holiday flats, one designed for the use of wheelchairs. These are proving a popular venue for those seeking a break in a peaceful rural area.

A remote cottage, Cwrt-Llacha, surrounded by trees and approached previously only on foot, has been delightfully modernised and now has vehicular access. Whilst some dwellings have been modernised beyond all recognition others have practically disappeared leaving only a heap of stones as evidence.

Additional dwellings have been built and today many people travel to work outside the area. The children attend schools in Usk, Shirenewton, Chepstow, Caerleon and Monmouth, some using LEA transport, others being transported by their parents. The local primary schools of Llangwm and Devauden closed in the 1980s.

What was the rectory is now a private dwelling and the church is one of five churches in the Llangwm group of parishes being served by the rector residing in the rectory at Gwernesney.

The former Plough Inn has also undergone many changes, from an inn to a farm – Pen-y-Bryn, a private dwelling, a country hotel and now a private dwelling again. Similarly Tredean Mansion has now been sold off from its land and woodlands. Undoubtedly there are many more changes on the way.

Index